# The Potting Bench

# The Potting Bench

## 60 Daily Garden Devotions
### *with the Master Gardener*

## Beth Fortune

# The Potting Bench

*60 Daily Garden Devotions with the Master Gardener*



Published by
Illumify Media Global
www.IllumifyMedia.com
*"Let's bring your book to life!"*

Paperback ISBN: 978-1-970582-06-2
Hardcover ISBN: 978-1-970582-09-3

Typeset by Art Innovations (http://artinnovations.in/)
Cover design by Debbie Lewis

*Printed in the United States of America*

# CONTENTS

# INTRODUCTION

"I love dirt under my nails, in my socks, on my clothes. Playing in God's creation brings joy, peace, harmony, and love to my life."

"My garden is a therapy for me! Digging in the dirt relieves stress! In my garden, it's me, my flowers, and God. I talk, reflect, and hum as I work. Perennials remind me every spring that we can all have new life and new beginnings each day."

The answers kept pouring in when I asked my gardening friends to share their favorite reasons for gardening.

"I love seeing something alive grow. God designed seeds and flowers and life cycles, and it's so cool to put a plant in the ground, and then it does its thing."

"Gardening has taught me patience. The rewards come through perseverance and hard work, over several seasons. Gardening is definitely a work in progress, just like me!"

Then there's the one that makes me think of my potting bench. "Feeling the dirt sift through my fingers as I repot a flower or getting on my knees in the flower bed as my hands become one with the soil. This takes me to my happy place."

While writing this collection of devotions, I pondered the reasons my friends gave me as well as my own. For me, it's the time I spend at my potting bench, potting plants, planning, and dreaming. It's also a place where I spend time with the Master Gardener, allowing Him to till my heart, just as I put my hands in the dirt to prepare the soil for planting. It's in these moments that I see the wonders of nature and the truths of the Bible come together under His watchful eyes. He alone can fertilize my life to grow faith, water seeds that'll germinate love, as well as prune out the lies that want to overtake truth. The most important discovery of all is that He's always with me. He's always with you too.

Listening to conversations in the grocery check-out, scrolling through social media, or meeting with a friend over coffee, I'm becoming more aware of the discontent and disconnect others are experiencing. It seems we are cultivating fear instead of faith, watering seeds of hate instead of love, and nurturing lies instead of truth.

Becoming one of those people who complain and get discouraged can be easy; however, I find that as I spend time with my heavenly Father, He helps me deal with feelings of discontentment, disconnection, and disillusionment. Just like I spend time at my potting bench learning more about gardening, enjoying the feel of the dirt through my fingers, and becoming centered doing something that brings me joy, it's the same way when I spend time with the Master Gardener. He teaches me and helps me grow as I hold His Word in my hands and spend time with Him, becoming more centered and joyful.

As we go through these devotions, we'll see God in all areas of our lives. He's in the stillness of the garden as we rest on a garden bench—a place where we sit, meditate, and be still, for it's in the stillness God reminds us that He's God and we aren't.

He's with us when our hearts become hard and we begin to close ourselves off to Him. Just as we need to break up the hard soil in our gardens, we also need the Holy Spirit to break up the hard places in us. The Master Gardener wants to give us a new heart, and He will if we allow Him to.

He's the God of second chances who'll repurpose our lives as He heals the cracked places. In love, He'll correct us by pruning, just as we prune our plants to help them grow stronger. He'll also encourage our growth by removing issues in our lives that may take over, like weeds, and He'll guide us by placing our feet on a path that meanders like a garden path, but one in which He knows the destination.

Have you ever felt insignificant? I think we all have. We may feel we're being overlooked, but that's not how the Master Gardener sees us as He looks over His garden and His children. God finds delight in us, and He has a plan for us.

My gardening journey began in South Carolina, watching my grandmother and my dad bring beauty from the red clay in our area. Wanting to know more, I went on to study ornamental horticulture at Clemson University and, after earning my degree, worked for a national mail-order seed company, gaining experience with large commercial growers. Since then, I've shared my love and knowledge of horticulture by working at local garden centers, giving garden talks at churches, schools, and garden clubs, teaching workshops, and working as a landscape designer and garden consultant.

I'm a Christian writer and speaker with over thirty years of ministry experience, including being a pastor's wife and Bible teacher. I love combining my knowledge of horticulture with rich biblical truths to help others become rooted in Christ, cultivate joy, and sow grace. As a freelance writer, I write devotions and articles for a variety of publications, and as a speaker, I speak at women's events and conferences and lead workshops. I enjoy photography when I'm not digging in the dirt or digging in God's Word. Seeing God's creation through the lens of my camera or phone has become not only a hobby but a passion.

For 60 days, *The Potting Bench* will bring lessons from the Master Gardener for those who want to see the biblical truths and gardening principles intertwine like beautiful vines along a fence. Each devotion offers a verse to anchor the day, a story or gardening experience with a spiritual application, a prayer, a section to dig deeper into the Scriptures or devotion, and ends with me sharing a practical gardening tip as if we were talking over the fence. All photographs are original photographs taken by me in my garden or while visiting other gardens or places of interest in my area of South Carolina and the Southeast.

Whether you are a seasoned gardener, a weekend novice, or someone who appreciates a vase full of beautiful, fresh flowers in your kitchen, I invite you to join me as we cultivate a deeper relationship with the Master Gardener and His Son, Jesus Christ. It's an invitation I offer with a prayer.

*Dear Lord, thank you for this time You've ordained for this book to be read by these readers and hopefully future friends. Take these lessons You've given me, and as seeds are planted, I pray these truths about You are planted in hearts to encourage, teach, and bring comfort. You know each of us, for You're a personal God, and You love us with a love that knows no bounds. May we be changed not only by the words on these pages but also by the time we have spent with You. For it's in Your Son Jesus' name, I pray, amen.*

# 1

# A NEW BEGINNING

*For I know the plans I have for you, declares the LORD,*
*plans for welfare and not for evil, to give you a future and a hope.*
**(Jeremiah 29:11)**

Garden gates are intriguing to me. They lure and invite me to peek into the world beyond their frame. It doesn't matter if it's a weathered wooden gate secured by rusty hinges or an ornate wrought iron masterpiece standing as a sentinel guarding a valuable treasure—I long to see inside.

The gate allows me to catch a glimpse of what's past the entrance. It may be a field of wildflowers, a lush pathway winding around a bend out of sight, a beautiful, manicured garden surrounding statues and fountains, or a simple garden someone has tended with love and devotion. But I can only see a little of what's hidden, and that's where the intrigue comes in and the desire to see more.

It's the same with new beginnings. Glancing through the frame of today, I have a desire to see and experience what's ahead. Even though I can't see everything before me, I know the Master Gardener is already there, and He has a plan for me. Knowing this, I can walk in boldness and courage, just as Joshua did as he entered the promised land to possess what God had already given him and the Israelites.

My desire is that as I walk through the gate toward a new beginning, I'll be more intentional to follow the Master Gardener, for He alone can lead me into the future and the hope He has for me.

**PRAYER:** *Thank you, Lord, that You have plans for me and give me boldness and courage to walk into a new season with You as my guide.*

**DIGGING DEEPER:** Are you peeking through a gate and toward a new beginning? Maybe you have it all figured out, but perhaps you don't. Sometimes our new beginning is a step of faith toward something new that God wants to do in our lives. Or maybe it's a time to start over. Whatever is stirring in you, it's never too late to begin, and God is waiting to walk with you.

**OVER THE GARDEN FENCE:** Whether constructing a classic wooden gate, a rustic gate with charm, or an arbor gate, keep the purpose in mind: Is it for looks or security? Consider the style and match it to your garden's overall theme.

# 2

# WAIT AND WORK

*See how the farmer waits for the precious fruit of the earth.*

**(James 5:7)**

Many of us are familiar with Henry Wadsworth Longfellow's quote, "All things come round to him who will but wait." I don't know whether Mr. Longfellow had gardeners in mind when he wrote this, probably not, but we gardeners do spend a lot of time waiting. However, we don't just wait; we work while we wait. While we anticipate the sprouting of our seeds, we weed and water. We plant our bulbs and watch for them to emerge as we tend the soil above. The words wait and work go together.

What circumstances in your life are you expecting the Lord to work out on your behalf? What prayers do you need answered, or what dreams do you want to see become a reality? Are you spending your time sitting, or are you busy? I get it—waiting isn't easy—but maybe if we put into practice the gardening principle of working while we wait, we'll see those needs met, the prayers answered, and our dreams come true.

We don't wait and work alone. We have the assurance that our Master Gardener is with us. He never leaves us nor forsakes us (Hebrews 13:5). Through His strength we can do all things (Philippians 4:13).

**PRAYER:** *Lord, as I wait for You to move on my behalf, help me to work and be patient in the waiting.*

**DIGGING DEEPER:** I wanted to become a speaker for women's events. As I waited, I helped acquire speakers for my church's events. I wanted to be a devotion writer. I began attending writers' conferences, worked on my craft, and waited for opportunities. What are you waiting for, and how can you be working as you wait? Ask the Lord to give you creative ideas and place people in your path to help.

**OVER THE GARDEN FENCE:** Save those cardboard boxes and use them to help with controlling weeds. Break down boxes, place them in a single layer on the ground, then cover with three to six inches of compost. Water thoroughly. Your earthworms will thank you.

# 3

# CONTAINER GARDENING



*But our citizenship is in heaven.*
**(Philippians 3:20)**

Container gardening is a great way to bring plants into small spaces and add color to porches, patios, or other areas of your yard or garden. What can you plant in containers? Almost anything you'd want—a flowering shrub, a group of plants of the same kind, or a combination of plants.

Containers are temporary housing for plants. Container gardening is one of my favorite garden practices because I can be creative and experiment with a variety of different plants. I can design a small landscape by selecting contrasting colors or texture combinations. It can be as simple, exotic, tropical, whimsical, or formal as I want.

Often, I'll start plants in containers with the intention of moving them to another location. As plants mature, they can become root-bound and need to be replanted in the ground to give them more room to grow. We, too, are planted in temporary earthen vessels. Our bodies are our temporary home, and our Master Gardener has a place waiting for us in heaven, where our real citizenship is. We may thrive here, accomplishing His purpose as my plants do in their containers, all the while remembering our permanent home is in heaven. There we'll one day be replanted in a perfect place where our roots can flourish and we can live forever with our Creator.

**PRAYER:** *Lord, help me to keep my eyes on things above, heaven, where You're preparing my forever home.*

**DIGGING DEEPER:** We may have a permanent address listed on our driver's license, but in the context of eternity, it's our temporary home. We'll all leave this earth and spend eternity somewhere. If you have placed your trust in Jesus Christ and accepted His gift of salvation, He is preparing your permanent home in heaven where you'll live with Him forever. Have you made this decision? If you want to know more, take time to read "A Note from Beth" at the end of this book, where I explain how to have the assurance that you'll go to heaven, your forever home.

**OVER THE GARDEN FENCE:** When planting in containers, make sure there's proper drainage so water won't collect at the bottom and cause the roots to rot. Rocks and gravel are good, but they can make the container heavy. I use packing peanuts, plastic bottles, and empty plastic pots, to name a few.

4

# ROOTED AND ESTABLISHED

As you therefore have received Christ Jesus the Lord, so walk in Him,<br>
rooted and built up in Him and established in the faith.<br>
(Colossians 2:6–8 NKJV)

Have you ever purchased small plants in nursery cell packs? Those plastic propagation trays that growers use to grow plants from seeds. I think we all have. More times than I can count, I've brought home pretty plants in anticipation of watching them grow, only to pull them out of the cell pack to discover they don't have an established root system.

When this happens, I leave the young plants in the trays while I feed and nurture them a little longer. When their roots are more mature, I'll transplant them into the ground or into containers with a greater chance of survival.

We can be like these young, immature plants when we aren't rooted and anchored in Jesus. Our enemy is always looking for ways to distract us from our walk with Him and make us ineffective. Just as I fed and nurtured my plants, we, too, need to be fed and nurtured by our Master Gardener. He alone, through His Word, can help us become rooted and established in our faith.

**PRAYER:** *Lord, help me to find more time to spend with You, growing deep roots of faith as I study Your Word.*

**DIGGING DEEPER:** Sometimes I wonder why God isn't using me more or why I'm not being promoted when I think I'm ready to move forward. It can happen to us all, no matter what stage of life we're in. Maybe we should stop and examine ourselves to see whether we have spent time maturing as a Christian, building strong roots of faith, so that we can be used. As we look to see whether our plants' roots are healthy before planting, so God does with us.

**OVER THE GARDEN FENCE:** When selecting plants, it's a good idea to pop them out of their containers and check the root system. Sometimes they can be root-bound if they've been left in the pot too long, or they may be so young they haven't had time to establish strong roots.

# 5

# USING OUR GIFTS

*As each one has received a gift, minister it to one another,*
*as good stewards of the manifold grace of God.*
**(1 Peter 4:10)**

The seeds arrived in a small brown envelope with a ribbon tied at the top. On the front was the name of the seeds, when and how to sow them, and when the flowers would bloom. The creative packaging from my dear friend was almost too cute to open, but I wanted to grow the beautiful and interesting hyacinth bean vine she was sharing with me.

And I'm glad I did open it and plant the seeds, for the vine did not disappoint. From the purple stems, green leaves, and purple flowers to the waxy purple seed pods, this fast-growing vine was a delight to watch for months. But I couldn't have enjoyed it without opening the package, planting the seeds, and following the directions.

It's the same with the gifts our Master Gardener gives us. We can go through our lives with our gifts closed in the proverbial seed packets sitting on a shelf instead of opening them, planting the seeds, and allowing them to grow. He has given us our gifts to be a blessing to others. He also plans to reward us for how we use them. Let's make sure we use the unique gifts we've been given, and as we sow, we'll also reap a blessing and bring glory to God.

**PRAYER:** *Lord, help me use the gifts You gave me to bless others and bring glory to You.*

**DIGGING DEEPER:** Do you know what your spiritual gift is? Many people even have more than one. You can find spiritual gift inventories available through churches or online to help you determine your gifts. Once you understand what the spiritual gifts are and recognize which one is yours, you can begin to use it, or them, to serve the Lord. Be careful not to be envious of another person's gift. God knows us best and knows which gifts He wants each one of us to have and how He wants us to use them to serve the world for Him.

**OVER THE GARDEN FENCE:** Planting seeds directly in the ground is often the best and easiest way. Make sure the soil is loose and well-draining. Follow the seed packet for depth and spacing. Keep weeds out and thin seedlings as they grow.

# 6

# HELLO SPRING

*For everything there is a season, and a time for every matter under heaven.*
**(Ecclesiastes 3:1)**

Scanning familiar places in my garden, I watch for old friends to reappear from their winter naps. I watch for them, awed by their tenacity and resilience. Some unfold as the fiddleheads of my ferns, and others break through the soil with old leaves and debris attached to their delicate stems as if they're holding on for more sleep. The plants may have looked dead, but they weren't, because their roots were protected and nourished under the soil.

At times, I resemble my beloved perennials—I've been planted, served a purpose, and then death arrives, so it seems. The barrenness sets in like the cold winds of winter. Maybe we've all had these same feelings. How do we survive these still and barren times? How do we combat the enemy, who wants to keep us from experiencing our breakthrough and another productive period?

Remember, it's a season. During the dark, quiet time, keep feeding your spirit, for your roots need nourishment. Live by faith, not by sight. Rejoice because the Master Gardener watches over us until we have our breakthrough. It will come, for there is "a time for every matter under heaven."

**PRAYER:** *Lord, help me remember that just because I may not see any evidence of something happening in my life doesn't mean it won't. By faith, I believe I'll have productive days again.*

**DIGGING DEEPER:** When spring arrives, take time to notice the plants sprouting up from the ground and let hope take root in your soul. Just as Jesus Christ died on the cross, was buried in a tomb, and then rose again to new life, we, too, can be resurrected to new life.

**OVER THE GARDEN FENCE:** A good time to divide overcrowded perennials is when they begin to emerge from the soil. Use a sharp-edged shovel to divide, making sure it's deep enough to split the roots.

# 7

# SHOW ME

*Even a child is known by his deeds.*
**(Proverbs 20:11 NKJV)**

"Show me your garden, and I shall tell you who you are." After reading that Alfred Austin was a poet and gardener himself, I think he was on to something when he wrote this line. As a consultant, I've seen many gardens—large, small, and every size in between. I can tell a lot about a person from their garden. I can tell what their favorite colors are by seeing a blanket of Rudbeckia daisies, yellow yarrow, or coreopsis. Or maybe they use more pastels, incorporating the soft pinks of peonies or bubblegum super petunias. I can also pick up on whether they like a formal look, a naturalistic look, or the whimsy of a cottage garden.

As I can tell a lot about a person by their garden, the Master Gardener reminds us that others can tell who we are by what they see in us. If "even a child is known by his deeds," how much more are we as adults known by our deeds? I think about this when I show impatience in the grocery line or with a server when I want more sweet tea while dining at a restaurant.

How about you? What are people seeing in you? We're walking testimonies, either of God's grace or of our self-centeredness. Think about this truth, whether you're tidying up your flower border, driving to work, or spending time with family or friends. People do watch and know more about you than you realize.

**PRAYER:** *Lord, help me remember that others are watching me and my actions and that I need to show others I'm Yours through my deeds.*

**DIGGING IN THE DIRT:** Oh, how easy it is to go through our days not being mindful of how others are watching us. Do you notice people's actions? Are you quick to judge? How do you think others see you? What are you showing others about yourself that you don't even realize? We need to remember that if a child is known by his deeds, so are we.

**OVER THE GARDEN FENCE:** One of the most popular landscape design elements is color. Before purchasing plants, hold them up next to each other to see if their colors complement. When planting at home, remember reds, oranges, and yellows look best in sunny locations. Cool colors, such as blues, purples, and greens, are more effective in shady areas. When designing a border, use the same color repeatedly to create a cohesive effect.

# 8

# HARD SOIL-HARD HEARTS

*And I will give you a new heart, and a new spirit I will put within you.*
**(Ezekiel 36:26)**

Have you ever watched large bulldozers and excavators clear land? Or a bucket-wheel excavator on a construction site? These pieces of equipment are huge, but they get the job done. I don't need this heavy equipment in my yard, but sometimes I feel as though I need something big to help me dig and break up the hard red clay in my area.

Water can run off our dry, hard soil before it soaks into the ground and reaches the roots to help them grow, and so can the Spirit of God run off our hard, dry hearts. In a spiritual sense, our hearts can become hardened to the point that we close ourselves off to God and the truths written in the Bible. What can cause this? Sin, pride, disappointments in life, and unforgiveness, to name a few. Do you deal with any of these? If you do, the Master Gardener is waiting to help. As a matter of fact, He wants to go a step further and replace your heart with a new one.

With a new heart, we can repent of our sin and pride, work through our disappointments, and forgive others. We can't do this in our own strength, and in the same way we need help breaking up the hard soil in our gardens, we need the Holy Spirit to break up the hard places in our hearts. The Master Gardener wants to do this wonderful work in our lives, but we need to allow Him to do it.

**PRAYER:** *Lord, I'm thankful that You want to give me a new heart and put a new spirit within me.*

**DIGGING DEEPER:** We can find many scriptures in the Old and New Testaments that tell us we should examine ourselves. Do you feel unmoved by the Word of God? Are you harboring bitterness or unforgiveness? Do you find yourself being less compassionate and more negative? These could be signs of a hardened heart. If you think yours has hardened, spend time alone with God and ask Him for a new one. He longs to give you one, if only you will ask.

**OVER THE GARDEN FENCE:** To correct hard soil, loosen it with a garden fork and remove debris. Then spread with compost, which adds organic matter. Mix in worm casting and bonemeal. Blend well, water, then wait a few days before planting.

# 9

# GROWING STRONG IN CHRIST

*But grow in the grace and knowledge of our Lord and Savior Jesus Christ.*
**(2 Peter 3:18)**

If one memory is seared in many parents' minds, it's the one of their children reaching up to offer a bouquet of freshly picked dandelions. How could they resist picking them? Those bright yellow flowers that grow no matter what we do to get rid of them are lovely.

Once I found out that dandelions are among the first flowers to bloom and serve as a primary food source for spring bees, I began to leave them alone. However, there are times they must be removed. You know where I'm going if you've tried to pull up one of these hardy plants. They have a sturdy root system, and if you don't pull up all the roots, they will grow back.

If the Master Gardener could choose a plant as an example of how our faith should be, I think it would be the dandelion with its bright yellow flowers. We need to grow and be rooted in God's Word so when the storms of life try to uproot us, we'll be as hard to remove as these resilient plants. Our spiritual roots should grow so deep into Christ that even if we are hit, we will survive.

And while we're growing those deep roots, we'll be a blessing to others, reminiscent of the versatile, life-giving source of the bright yellow flowers our children can't resist.

**PRAYER:** *Lord, help me to grow deep roots in Christ so I can stay strong when trials of this life want to destroy me.*

**DIGGING DEEPER:** Life is full of surprises. Sometimes our lives can come crashing down with one phone call, a visit, or a letter. I've been there. It took one phone call to change my world when my mother called to tell me a spot was discovered on my dad's lung after a routine exam. The Bible is full of verses we can rely on when we're hit with life's trials and troubles. Would you like more stability, joy, and nourishment? Begin to find more time to explore God's Word. Choose a topic or word to study. Or choose a book of the Bible to start exploring. Then, when a surprise comes your way, your roots will have grown deep and strong.

**OVER THE GARDEN FENCE:** Are there times when you want to remove some dandelions from your flower beds? The best way to remove them is by hand while the soil is wet. Make sure you remove the entire tap root, or it will return.

# 10

# FROM FROST TO FLOURISHING

*Be not dismayed, for I am your God; I will strengthen you, I will help you.*
**(Isaiah 41:10)**

ardeners can't wait for the first sunny spring day to head to their favorite garden center. Having worked at one, I can tell you it doesn't take much of a rise on the thermometer for the parking lot to fill up. Pulling their wagons, I'd watch our customers ignore the "Beware of Late Frost" signs strategically placed around the center until after April 15 as they reached for new treasures.

There was more than one occasion when it was all hands on deck for employees at the end of the day, while we covered rows and rows of tender bedding plants with cheesecloth and sheets to protect them from possible freezing temperatures. Over the years, you've probably taken a sheet and covered a budding shrub or row of freshly planted annuals. I get it: We don't care how it looks to our neighbors; we want to protect our plants from a setback due to frost. But these cold events are as unwelcome as trials are undesirable in our lives.

Can you relate? You've planned and prepared, and life is going great. Then an unforeseen circumstance comes upon you and sets you back. When a plant is hit by frost, it'll slow the growth down, but what survives will be stronger. It's the same with us. The Master Gardener uses our setbacks and our disappointments to strengthen our faith. Isaiah reminds us not to be dismayed but to remember God is with us and will strengthen us so we will flourish.

**PRAYER:** *Lord, I thank You for always being with me during life's unwelcomed trials and for making me stronger as I go through them.*

**DIGGING DEEPER:** Trials can be hard enough, but when they're unexpected, they're even more challenging to handle. Go ahead and prepare for them now. How? By learning more about the nature of God and His unwavering love for us, and by memorizing Scripture. Our faith will be strong when we need it.

**OVER THE GARDEN FENCE:** As you become aware of frost warnings, water plants to strengthen them and water the ground to retain heat. Then cover tender plants with breathable material such as cheesecloth, a sheet, or frost cloth before nightfall.

# 11

# ABIDING

*I am the vine; you are the branches. Whoever abides in me and I in him,*
*he it is that bears much fruit, for apart from me you can do nothing.*
**(John 15:5)**

She was beautiful and the focal point of the yard. My blooming and thriving clematis—the "queen of climbers," they're called—had exceeded my expectations. I'd trained her thin leafy stems to grow up and twist along an old tractor wheel, and it was stunning. If this was how she looked in two years of growth, I couldn't wait to see how many blooms she would produce next year.

Then it happened, the unthinkable. In a lapse of judgment on a warm day, while I was pruning other plants, I noticed some thin, brown wood around the tractor wheel. Well, that needed to go too, I thought, and in a hasty moment I began cutting the brown, unwanted stems.

Fast-forward a few hours, and I noticed all the green leaves around the brown stems were dying. Then it hit me: I'd severed the branches from the vine, its life source.

Nothing illustrates the principle taught in John 15 better than what I did that warm spring day. When I cut the branches away from the vine, it could no longer bear fruit or bloom, for without the vine, it could not do anything.

As we live to please the Master Gardener, we need to learn to abide in Christ daily because we, the branches, can't bear fruit—or do anything—without Christ, the vine.

**PRAYER:** *I thank You, Jesus, that You're my life source. Help me to abide in You so I can live and bear fruit.*

**DIGGING DEEPER:** As a branch depends on the vine for nourishment, we, too, need to rely upon Jesus, the vine, for our spiritual nourishment. How many times do we try to live the Christian life in our own strength? We struggle, experience defeat, and become weary. We must have an intimate relationship with Jesus Christ, the source of life that enables us to produce spiritual fruit for His glory.

**OVER THE GARDEN FENCE:** Want to grow clematis? Choose a sunny location with well-drained soil for the most blooms. The roots prefer cool conditions and need to be shaded by the plant itself or covered with leaves or compost. Provide a trellis that's less than a quarter inch in diameter since leaf stems are short.

# 12

# QUIET MOMENTS

*The whole earth is at rest and quiet; they break forth into singing.*

**(Isaiah 14:7)**

Truman Capote once said, "In my garden, after a rainfall, you can faintly, yes, hear the breaking of new blooms."

It was a quiet moment—a moment after a rain shower in the mountains. Walking along the brick pathway, enjoying the beauty of the flowers on both sides of me, I watched the raindrops hang on, as if taking a breath, before falling to the ground. As I watched, I, too, wanted to hold my breath.

Such peace and beauty surrounded by majestic mountains and silence. Pulling my camera to my eye and aiming to take a photo, it was as if I could hear the breaking of a new bloom. A miracle that happens all the time, but I don't stop to notice. I did stop that day, and I try to remember to do the same after it rains.

It's the same when I spend time with the Master Gardener. With Him I walk along the pathway of words from the Bible, and I find myself wanting to hold my breath as I stop to notice the love He has for us, His children, and the miracles all around us.

Take time to spend with the Lord today. The more time you do, the more miracles you'll see, and they may even take your breath away.

**PRAYER:** *Lord, forgive me for being so busy that I don't stop to make time to spend with You and read Your word.*

**DIGGING DEEPER:** In Isaiah 14, God promised Israel would be restored after He destroyed their enemies, and they would have a time of rest and quiet. He promises us rest and quiet too. And one day our enemy, Satan, will be destroyed. Until then, God gives us the strength to endure hardships and trials. Put your hope in the Lord today, no matter what you're facing, and look for the miracles of His enduring love all around you.

**OVER THE GARDEN FENCE:** Can plants be stressed? Yes. Common reasons are poor soil, too much fertilizer, not enough water, the temperature being either too hot or too cold. Pay attention—your plants will let you know, the same as people do when they are stressed.

# 13

# GOD'S MASTERPIECE

*For we are his workmanship.*

**(Ephesians 2:10)**

"I miss seeing your dad working in his beautiful yard."

I heard this statement often when my dad died after losing his battle with lung cancer at the age of sixty-four. He had a lovely yard—lush green lawn, colors that popped, and a stunning rose garden for my mom surrounded by a split rail fence he'd constructed himself.

Each season was a masterpiece of his unyielding work, but that first spring he was unable to put on his mud-caked brogans and get into his yard, neglect began to show. By summer, our broken hearts weren't the only evidence of our loss; his yard revealed his absence too. As hard as my mother, my brothers, and I tried, we couldn't do what he had done.

As his yard became untidy and out of control when my dad was no longer in it, the same can happen to our lives if we don't let the Master Gardener be part of it. We are His workmanship, His masterpiece, and our lives are the evidence of His tender, loving care. He doesn't want to be held at arm's length. No, He wants to be weaving in and out of our lives, decisions, relationships, and plans, just as my dad weaved in and out of his flower beds and rose garden.

**PRAYER:** *Lord, I'm so thankful that I'm Your masterpiece and that You desire to tend and care for me.*

**DIGGING DEEPER:** Daily, I must allow God to come into my life to feed, prune, train, and care for me. If not, my life will begin to look unkept like my dad's neglected yard. What about you? Do you allow God to be a part of your life? Do you spend time with Him, reading His Word, praying, and serving Him? As hard as I try, I can't do what God can do in and through me, for I am His masterpiece, and so are you.

**OVER THE GARDEN FENCE:** Biennials need extra effort to grow, but they are well worth it. They complete their life cycle in two years. In the first year, leaves are produced; in the second year, flowers appear. Then the plant needs to be replanted. You won't regret growing Canterbury bells, Sweet William, hollyhocks, or foxgloves, to name a few.

# 14

# PULLING WEEDS

*See to it . . . that no "root of bitterness" springs up and causes trouble.*
**(Hebrews 12:15)**

Say the word *gardening*, and you'll get an "aah" response. Say the word *weeding*, and the "aah" can turn into an "ugh." But as any seasoned gardener knows, the weeds are going to come. And they'll take over and ruin the most manicured and thriving bed if they're not removed in a timely manner.

Tools are available to help with weeding, but getting our gloved hands in the soil, yanking out the uninvited guests by the roots, and throwing them away is best. If we don't remove the root, we know the weed will come back and cause trouble.

When it comes to our Master Gardener taking care of us, He knows all too well we need the weeds of our lives removed by the roots. One of the weeds we deal with is bitterness. The writer of Hebrews refers to a root of bitterness as any unresolved hurt, anger, or resentment we harbor.

As we don't want weeds around our flowers to choke out the beauty we've created and destroy the purpose of our garden, our Master Gardener feels the same about us, His creation. He wants us to bloom, be fruitful, and mature into what He has created us to be. If you're dealing with bitterness, won't you ask God to remove it today? Rest assured, He won't yank it out; He'll remove it gently, with love.

**PRAYER:** *Lord, show me if I have any bitterness that needs to be removed by Your gentle and loving hands so I can have Your peace in my life.*

**DIGGING DEEPER:** Are you holding on to any past hurts, resentment, anger, or bitterness? Look carefully and ask the Lord to help you resolve them so they don't cause you pain. Confess the presence of the bitterness, choose to forgive those who have caused you pain, and then ask God to heal the wounds of your heart.

**OVER THE GARDEN FENCE:** To make pulling weeds easier, water the soil first, then reach down to the soil line and grip the weed at the base. Pull gently so you will pull up the root along with the weed. It's always best to pull up weeds as soon as you see them, before they set seeds that will grow more weeds.

# 15

# SPIRITUAL LESSON FROM THE GARDEN

*A disciple is not above his teacher, but everyone when he is fully trained will be like his teacher.*
**(Luke 6:40)**

Each time I turn the soil with my trowel to loosen it and add a new plant to my garden or containers, I find myself thanking the Master Gardener for showing me spiritual lessons. I've found that what's true in the garden holds true in my spiritual life.

Watering—Sprinkling a little water on plants is not watering. The soil needs to be soaked to provide adequate moisture to penetrate the dry soil. Likewise, we need a good soaking of Christ every day. He is the living water, and the more we accept His love and follow Him, the more we will be filled with abundant joy. A joy as refreshing as a summer rain.

Weeding—Weeding is an ongoing chore. Just when I think I've pulled the last pesky weed, a week or two later I find more weeds to pull. Weeding sin out is also an ongoing chore. When I think I've eradicated sin, another one wants to rise to the surface. Even as the weeds in my garden can take over a flower bed and choke out the desired plants, sin can take over the Christ-like attributes I want others to see in me.

Pruning—Damaged and diseased stems and branches must be removed to keep plants healthy. It's the same in my life. I need to prune damaged or diseased areas from my life, such as unhealthy relationships, activities that take me away from more important responsibilities, or circumstances that keep my focus off my Christian walk.

Feeding—Plants need nutrients. They can become weak and die without proper nutrition, and I'm no different. It's vital I feed my spirit by studying God's Word, fellowshipping with other Christians, and spending time in prayer.

**PRAYER:** *Lord, help me become spiritually healthy by following the spiritual lessons I see in my garden. Your Word is my delight as I follow You today.*

**DIGGING DEEPER:** It's easy to forget to take care of ourselves spiritually. Where are you falling short right now? Are you spending time with Jesus, our living water? Are you ignoring a correcting nudge from the Holy Spirit about issues that need to be pulled out or pruned? What about studying God's Word? We can all take time to inventory our spiritual well-being.

**OVER THE GARDEN FENCE:** Want to sound like a smart gardener? Here's a new word: *hydrozoning*. It's the practice of grouping together plants with the exact same water needs. Most of us are already hydrozoning and don't even realize it.

# 16

# BIRDS AND BLUEBERRIES

*He who is in you is greater than he who is in the world.*

**(1 John 4:4)**

*I* enjoy my birds, and I love blueberries. I like to feed my birds, but I don't like feeding them my blueberries. However, that's precisely what happens when my blueberries start growing on the bush: The birds think the fruits are for them. What do I do to keep them away? I drape bird netting over the plant to keep the birds from eating the berries before I can harvest them to make a topping for our morning cereal or blueberry muffins.

It's the same with our enemy, Satan. He wants to swoop down and rob us of our fruit or keep us from producing at all. He does this by speaking lies into our minds and hearts, trying to get us to believe them. However, we have a spiritual net that's stronger than any net I use to keep my birds away.

If we ask, the Master Gardener will provide a covering over us so the Enemy can't penetrate. He can keep the Enemy from swooping down and speaking lies into our minds and hearts. He can also heal the wounds that may have been caused by neglect in preparing for the Enemy.

Yes, if I forget my net, my blueberries can be gone in a few days. When we neglect our time with the Lord and don't let Him cover us with His Word, we can also lose our fruit. Our Master Gardener created birds, blueberries, you, and me. And I can tell you, He loves us more and will fight to protect us.

**PRAYER:** *Dear Lord, help me to remember to spend time with You, allowing You to cover me and protect me from my enemy, Satan.*

**DIGGING DEEPER:** We can learn to resist the devil, and as the Bible says, he will flee from us. God gives us the strength to do this when we ask Him. Don't battle the enemy alone; lean on the Lord and His Word to lead, guide, and protect. God is a prayer away.

**OVER THE GARDEN FENCE:** The ideal soil pH for blueberries is 4.8–5.2. Plant in the spring or fall, and wait a month before fertilizing so the plants can get established. When you see new growth, use an acidic fertilizer, such as that used for azaleas and rhododendrons. Add mulch to protect shallow roots, prevent weeds, and hold moisture.

# 17

# GARDEN APRONS

*Therefore, as the elect of God, . . .*
*put on tender mercies, kindness, humility, meekness, longsuffering.*
**(Colossians 3:12 NKJV)**

Every gardener loves a good apron, whether it's a bib or a waist apron. We look for ones that are durable, lightweight, comfortable, and, if possible, washable. And lots of pockets. We set out to work in our gardens, prepared with our hats, gloves, and tools, ready for whatever needs to be done. And thanks to the apron, we can carry a lot with us.

Our Master Gardener has given us tools to use in our daily lives, and He wants us to have them ready and available like the tools we carry in our aprons: tender mercies, kindness, humility, meekness, longsuffering. No, we don't need these exact tools for deadheading our zinnias or training our climbing rose along a trellis, but we do need them when we leave the garden and get around people.

As we look further in Colossians, we see the tools we carry in our spiritual apron aren't for us but for "bearing with one another, and forgiving one another" (Colossians 3:13), in other words, making allowances for others' faults and forgiving those who offend us. We need to be equipped because we don't know what we'll need at any given moment.

Next time you head out to a family gathering, church event, work, or to run an errand, don't forget your spiritual apron, because you're probably going to need something from it. And make sure you have the kind with plenty of pockets.

**PRAYER:** *Lord, help me to remember to take my spiritual apron with me today so I'll be equipped with tender mercies, kindness, humility, meekness, and longsuffering.*

**DIGGING DEEPER:** As I read Colossians 3:12, I can feel overwhelmed about what God is asking of me. Some days I can do it with ease, but on others I find it much more difficult. It's at these times that I must dig deeper and ask God for help. As I begin my morning prayer, I've started incorporating a request for God to bring others in my path where I can put these tools to use and, at the end of the day, give Him all the glory for the outcome.

**OVER THE GARDEN FENCE:** Two of my favorite apron styles are bib and waist aprons. I use the bib style when potting plants at my potting bench or a waist-high table because I get soil everywhere. The waist apron is my go-to apron when pruning, deadheading, or weeding in my flower beds. And all with plenty of pockets, of course.

# 18

# BLOOM DESTROYERS

*And let us not grow weary of doing good, for in due season we will reap,*
*if we do not give up.*
**(Galatians 6:9)**

"What have y'all done? Those are my daylilies I've cross-pollinated!"

Cross-pollinated. My brothers and cousins had no idea what my grandmother was talking about as she ran toward them. They didn't know whether to drop their sticks and run or stay and face the music—again. It wasn't the first time they'd gotten into my grandmother's flower beds and destroyed some of her prized plants while playing games. This time, they'd popped and destroyed every swollen daylily flower bud they could find.

My grandmother loved her daylilies. Each year when the flowers opened, she'd hand-pollinate them, collect the seeds, plant them, then wait for the new varieties to grow and bloom. It was a long process that took an entire year to bear fruit from her labor. Now, because of her grandsons' antics, she would have to start over.

This can happen to us: We can pour into a project, work diligently on an idea, and when we think our efforts are about to bloom or produce, an unexpected life event comes along and destroys what we were working on. We never get to see what we could have accomplished. What my brothers and cousins did that day didn't deter my grandmother. She began again. The following year, when the flowers opened, she cross-pollinated and waited a year to see the fruit of her labor. I'm sure when she saw the new colors of flowers she had created, she became even more excited. They had survived not only the winds and the rain but also her grandchildren.

**PRAYER:** *Father, help me not to give up but to persevere and keep moving forward, so my dreams are not destroyed.*

**DIGGING DEEPER:** Has there been a time in your life when you worked hard on a project or toward a goal only to have it destroyed? What have you worked on that's unfinished due to external factors? Did you begin again? I hope so. Don't grow weary or become discouraged because in due season you'll reap your reward.

**OVER THE GARDEN FENCE:** To cross-pollinate daylilies, first select the two flowers you want to cross. Find the pollen from one flower and place it on the tip of the pistil of the other flower, and then harvest the seeds (between forty and sixty days). Plant the seeds, wait, and if you have grandsons with sticks, make sure you protect the flowers so they can have a chance to bloom.

# 19

# HE KNOWS OUR NAME

*Fear not, for I have redeemed you; I have called you by name, you are mine.*

**(Isaiah 43:1)**

Labels are an invaluable item to gardeners. We use them to mark the location of seeds we've sown and label new plants so we can remember their names. Labels come in a variety of materials, from the generic white plastic pieces we write on with a marker to very ornate, attractive ones made of wood or metal offered at specialty shops.

No matter what type we use, we want to keep track of all our seedlings and plants in their new homes in our flower beds or gardens. We may forget the name of one of our beauties, but not our Master Gardener. You will not see Him with a white piece of plastic and a marker or an ornate label walking through His garden writing down names of His children so He won't forget. For He always knows each one of us by name.

How do I know? Because in Jeremiah 1:5 God said, "Before I formed you in the womb, I knew you." God formed us, and He knew us before we were born. How can He not know our name?

May we walk in the assurance that no matter what happens today, God knows our name, He sees us, and He cares for us.

**PRAYER:** *Thank you, Father, that You created me and You know me by name. I am Your child, and You will always be with me.*

**DIGGING DEEPER:**  What a tremendous promise we read in Scripture that God calls us by name. But that's not the only promise. According to Revelation 2:17 (NKJV), "To him who overcomes I will give some of the hidden manna to eat. And I will give him a white stone, and on the stone a new name written which no one knows except him who receives it." Yes, one day we will receive a new name from God, one He has selected only for us. Think on this today. We have a personal God who loves us and has a name He has chosen waiting on us.

**OVER THE GARDEN FENCE:** I've found the best labels that'll work from year to year are metal ones you mark with a permanent Sharpie. Plastic labels can become brittle and break, while wooden ones can become wet, causing them to rot before the end of the year.

# 20

# GOD'S TIMING

*Be still before the LORD and wait patiently for him.*
**(Psalm 37:7)**

"Adopt the pace of nature: her secret is patience," as Ralph Waldo Emerson said. Patience is something all gardeners could use more of as we wait for seedlings to sprout, leaves to grow, and flowers to bloom. Even after all these years of tilling the soil, planting new additions to my garden, and tending the existing ones, I'm still impatient when it comes to anticipating the first blooms of the year. I want *my* timing, not nature's timing.

My impatience rolls over into my spiritual life much as my actual impatiens plant spills over the edge of my strawberry jar. I want to see results in my life, and I want my own timing, not the Lord's. Psalm 37:7 tells us we need to "rest in the LORD and wait patiently . . ." Rest in the Lord. That's difficult for me because I'm not wired that way. I want to be doing something to help the Lord.

I'm learning I can't hurry a flower to bloom any earlier than its time, and I can't move God along or put Him on my timetable either. I need to learn to rest in Him. When I do, I'll find peace in the waiting. The secret? Patience. Mr. Emerson uncovered a truth when he advised us to "adopt the pace of nature." I think I will take that one step further and remember not only to adopt the pace of nature but also to rest in the Lord. Now, that's a secret I need to share. It's not our timing we should seek but God's.

**PRAYER:** *Lord, help me to rest in You. And in my waiting, teach me patience.*

**DIGGING DEEPER:** What keeps you from resting in the Lord and waiting on His timing? Do you trust Him enough? In our fast-paced world, we're used to instant gratification, and waiting is a negative. How can you begin to see waiting for God and His timing as a positive? Think back on a time when God answered your prayer in His timing, and be encouraged, it was indeed perfect.

**OVER THE GARDEN FENCE:** Strawberry jars are fun containers. They can be planted with a variety of herbs, impatiens, pansies, violas, or strawberry plants in the fall and winter. Plant the lower openings first, then work your way up, and plant the top last.

# 21

# HEAVEN'S GARDEN

*To an inheritance that is imperishable, undefiled, and unfading, kept in heaven for you.*
**(1 Peter 1:4)**

We arrived early, camera bags on our shoulders, and our hearts happy to be visiting a nearby botanical garden. Walking along the rustic boardwalk, we could see the rays of the sun and the gentle shadows being cast before us. Off we went, each in our own direction, delighted to be in such a lovely place. So much color, and so many different plants and flowers. The more I aimed my camera, the more I realized the uniqueness of each one found planted in rows, nestled close in flower beds, or stretching across fences. I was experiencing a touch of heaven.

The Master Gardener promises a place even more lovely for those who have accepted His Son, Jesus. If we think places here on Earth are paradise, how much more wonderful will heaven be? John gives us a glimpse of our heavenly home in Revelation where he writes, "Then the angel showed me the river of the water of life, bright as crystal, flowing from the throne of God and of the Lamb through the middle of the street of the city; also, on either side of the river, the tree of life with its twelve kinds of fruit, yielding its fruit each month. The leaves of the tree were for the healing of the nations. No longer will there be anything accursed, but the throne of God and of the Lamb will be in it" (Revelation 22:1–3).

Think of this celestial place today. It's a place reserved for us that hasn't been corrupted and will never fade away. Now, that sounds like heaven.

**PRAYER:** *Father, thank You for the promise of heaven where we'll be with You, Jesus, and our loved ones for eternity.*

**DIGGING DEEPER:** I've heard people say we shouldn't be so heavenly minded that we aren't of any earthly good. I understand their point. We need to live in the here and now, sharing our testimonies and leading others to Christ. However, that doesn't mean we can't also be looking for His appearing and for our future home in heaven. I think it's more like this: If we are heavenly minded, we will be of more earthly good.

**OVER THE GARDEN FENCE:** Use plants with variegated foliage to bring interest to your garden. Choose plants with a variety of colors and patterns, but use them sparingly to get a more dramatic effect.

# 22

# THE FRAGRANT GARDEN

*For we are to God the fragrance of Christ among those who are being saved and among those who are perishing.*

**(2 Corinthians 2:15 NKJV)**

Boyce Tankersley was quoted as saying, "Fragrance adds an extra layer of richness to the landscape." Years ago, I had the opportunity to visit a friend's vegetable and herb garden. Walking along one of the pathways, I tilted my head upward because riding on the breeze was the loveliest scent. Before I could ask, she answered, "It's jasmine. The vines are planted beside the house."

Being greeted outside with the scent of jasmine, roses, honeysuckle, or the sweet, floral smell of gardenias can be a pleasant surprise. It's a wonderful idea to incorporate plant material that fills the air with unforgettable scents. And it can be so welcoming to use fragrant plants placed in containers near the front door or planted along walkways for your guests to enjoy.

Paul reminds us that to the Master Gardener we're the fragrance of Christ. We aren't the source of the fragrance, but we carry the fragrance of Christ among the people we meet. If we are Christ followers, we are giving off the scent of the fruit of the Spirit found in Galatians 5:22–23—love, joy, peace, patience, kindness, goodness, faithfulness, gentleness, and self-control. We also give off a life-giving aroma when we share the hope we've found in Christ.

Next time we smell the perfumed fragrance of Hyacinthus in the spring or the pleasant scent of sweet alyssum, which even the pollinators can't resist, we should stop and ask ourselves if we're carrying the fragrance of Christ to those we meet. We may even cause them to stop for a moment and tilt their head upward. Then we can answer, "It's Jesus. He's planted in my heart."

**PRAYER:** *Lord, help me to carry the fragrance of Christ to others by demonstrating the fruit of the Spirit.*

**DIGGING DEEPER:** When I catch a scent of a pleasing fragrance, whether in the garden or home, I want to know its source. May we become the fragrance of Christ to others—the source. To those who are saved, may we be an encouragement to them, and to those who are perishing, may we point them to Jesus.

**OVER THE GARDEN FENCE:** Scents in the garden most often come from flowers, but don't forget about certain foliage plants, including rosemary, lavender, balsam, and a variety of mint, to name a few.

# 23

# LESSON IN PRUNING

*Every branch in me that does not bear fruit he takes away, and every branch that does
bear fruit he prunes, that it may bear more fruit.*

**(John 15:2)**

Pruning is essential, but when should it be done? For most shrubs, it's in late winter or early spring before buds set. It's the same for fruit trees: They're pruned at this same time while they're dormant, before the sap begins to flow and there's new growth. And perennials? Springtime's best. Pruning is used to keep plants in shape, remove diseased and old limbs, and encourage new growth.

Our Master Gardener knows spiritual pruning is important for our growth too. We may not understand when He comes toward us with the shears of His love and discipline, but He knows when we need it. God removes the branches in us that don't produce fruit and cuts back fruit-producing branches to make them even more productive and stronger.

Do you want to grow spiritually? Do you want to bear more fruit? Do you want God to remove from you whatever isn't producing fruit in your life? I think we would all say yes, but that doesn't always mean it won't hurt. If it makes you anxious to think about being pruned, ask God to increase your faith. We are His children, and He does this because He loves us.

**PRAYER:** *Lord, help me to accept when pruning is needed in my life.*

**DIGGING DEEPER:** Are you dragging around dead branches? It could be old wounds, unhealthy relationships, or negative attitudes that are hurtful and keeping you from growing and bearing fruit. God wants to cut away those dead and diseased parts so you can live a joyful and abundant life. The process can be uncomfortable, but it'll be worth it to let God do the work. Pray about what could be hindering you and keeping you from bearing fruit.

**OVER THE GARDEN FENCE:** When pruning, always cut above an outward-facing bud to promote new growth. Use sharp, clean tools to prevent disease. Make sure you keep at least two-thirds of the plant each year.

# 24

# GOD PROVIDES

*Consider the lilies of the field, how they grow.*
**(Matthew 6:28)**

Looking out over the garden, everything we see, hear, smell, touch, or taste God created. From the smallest microorganism that's crucial for soil health and plant growth to the largest tree, they were made by Him. From a delicate bloom attached to a hosta stem to a striking dinnerplate dahlia. The sound of birds, the fragrance of lavender, the taste of peaches, the softness of lamb's ear growing in a perennial bed—they're all made by the Master Gardener.

We can forget this when we bolt out the door each day. We fly through our lives, watching the clock and moving from one activity to the next, like a hummingbird flitting from one bloom to another. We get weary; then worry is close behind.

Matthew reminds us we shouldn't worry. He uses clothing as an example of something we worry about it and compares it with the lilies of the field. He writes, "They neither toil nor spin . . . But if God so clothes the grass of the field, . . . will he not much more clothe you?" (Matthew 6:28–30). What a beautiful reminder, as we look over a field of wildflowers, a backyard vegetable garden, or a container of red geraniums on our back porch, that if God can create such beauty, He can care for us and provide for our needs.

Are you worrying about something or someone today? Are there situations and issues before you that bring anxiety because you don't have answers? Do you have a financial, physical, or emotional need today? If God provides for the wildflowers and lilies, which are temporary, how much more will He provide for you and me, who are of a much greater value to Him?

**PRAYER:** *Lord, I'm thankful You're my provider and care for me even more than Your creation.*

**DIGGING DEEPER:** Worry can scamper over our hearts to the point we lose sight of the fact that God is our provider. What provisions do you need today? Take a moment and pray, talking to God about your needs. Ask for wisdom and for Him to increase your faith as you wait on Him to move on your behalf or on behalf of someone you love.

**OVER THE GARDEN FENCE:** Want to feed your family from your garden? It can be as simple as growing lettuce in containers for year-round harvest, provided it is winter protected. Sow seeds in early spring to mid-fall, then harvest in late spring to late fall.

# 25

# WORDS OF WISDOM

*King Rehoboam rejected the advice of the elders.*
**(2 Chronicles 10:13 NKJV)**

"I wouldn't plant that there if I were you."

"But I want it near my door so I can see it."

My friend couldn't resist planting a wisteria vine near her front door so she could enjoy the fragrant purple cluster of flowers. It was lovely as a young plant, but its stems kept growing until they were climbing up the side of the house and into the garage. If you've grown wisteria, you know what I'm talking about, but if you haven't, you may want to pay attention.

After a few weeks, she said, "I should have listened to you."

And she is still telling me this as she gets her pruning shears out year after year to keep it contained. I did try to warn her, as I'd learned from experience. I knew what the vine was capable of because I once had a beautiful wisteria vine take over a fence, climb a tree, and would have covered my forsythia shrub border had I not stopped it.

When we choose not to take the advice of those who have experienced more life than we have, we may end up learning some difficult lessons the hard way. The Bible is full of stories of people from whom we can learn and gain wisdom. And the Master Gardener puts people in our paths to help us if we will listen. And that gardening friend who tries to give advice, you may want to take note, especially if they're sharing from experience.

**PRAYER:** *Lord, help me to listen to those who are wiser or older than myself. If they're willing to share their experiences with me, let me be wise enough to learn from them.*

**DIGGING DEEPER:** Do you have someone in your life whom you can go to for guidance? Do you know of someone younger than you, either in years or spiritual maturity, to whom you could impart some of your wisdom? I once heard we all should have someone akin to apostle Paul in our lives, from whom we can seek counsel, and another person like his young friend Timothy, in whom we can share our wisdom. Ask God who these two people could be in your life.

**OVER THE GARDEN FENCE:** Grow wisteria the smart way—plant in full sun and in well-drained soil. Provide a strong structure, such as a trellis or arbor, for support, and prune frequently but lightly in the summer. Remove suckers from the base of the plant as they appear.

# 26

# TRUST THE PROCESS

*Trust in the L*ORD *with all your heart, and do not lean on your own understanding.*
**(Proverbs 3:5)**

always find it interesting how perennials die in the winter, then reappear as the soil and air begin to warm in the spring. Take peonies, for example; right now, my plant still has lush green leaves that will remain through the summer. However, a night is coming when temperatures will drop below freezing, and the entire aboveground plant will turn brown and die back.

During the winter months, the plant's roots will continue to grow and store nutrients while protected by the soil, allowing it to survive. When the ground warms, I'll see red tender shoots push through the soil, and leaves will grow until I once again have a lush green shrub with beautiful blooms in May. Year after year, this happens, and I've learned to trust the process.

Sometimes my life feels dormant. I read in the Bible that the Lord has plans for me, but here I sit—waiting. What about you? Are you there now? The writer of Proverbs reminds us we need to "Trust in the Lord with all your heart, and do not lean on your own understanding," and then he goes on to say, "In all your ways acknowledge Him, and he will make straight your paths" (Proverbs 3:6).

Dormancy doesn't mean nothing's going on under the soil, and it's the same when we are waiting on the Master Gardener to use us. We need to trust Him, acknowledge Him, and in His time, we will grow and bloom.

**PRAYER:** *Lord, help me to depend on You more, especially when I don't see anything happening in my life.*

**DIGGING DEEPER:** Trust the process. It's easier said than done, but we can be active in our waiting. If you find you're in a place of waiting, spend more time with the Lord. This time may be a gift you didn't realize you needed. A gift of time. If used wisely, you'll begin to see how God is teaching, preparing, and strengthening you for what He has next for you to do.

**OVER THE GARDEN FENCE:** When caring for peonies, in the fall, trim the plant back to the ground, right above the crown, after the leaves turn brown or yellow. This will allow the plant to begin storing energy for strong stems and blooms the following year. Afterward, lightly cover with mulch.

# 27

# GRAFTED IN

*And you, although a wild olive shoot, were grafted in among the others and now share in the nourishing root of the olive tree.*

**(Romans 11:17)**

Who doesn't love being the recipient of a vase of long-stem roses, the popular choice for Valentine's Day and anniversaries. And how enchanting and romantic it is walking through a rose garden, enjoying the beauty and fragrance of hybrid tea roses, the largest class of roses. These rose bushes are a cross between hybrid perpetual roses and tea roses, producing the high-centered blooms and long, sturdy stems we admire.

To provide this more vigorous and disease-resistant rose, it's common practice to graft the hybrid tea with the gorgeous blooms onto a hardy rootstock. Grafting a bud from a top-performing rose onto a rootstock ensures a strong, healthy stem and root system. Two parts exist—the aboveground part that produces the flowers and the belowground part that provides a resilient root system.

Using the practice of grafting, Paul shows how Gentile believers, the wild olive tree, are grafted into God's family, the olive tree. Gentiles weren't a part of the original family of God to obtain His covenants and promises that belonged to Abraham and his descendants. I'm thankful the Master Gardener provided a way for all to be included in His family. When Gentiles put their faith in Jesus Christ, they're grafted into God's family and can become much stronger, just as the hybrid tea roses are stronger on a healthy rootstock. Next time you're at the garden center, walk through the rose section to admire the velvety red of a "Mr. Lincoln" or the lovely scent of a "Peace" rose, remembering God loves you so much and He's made a way to graft you into His family.

**PRAYER:** *Lord, thank You for Your Son, Jesus. By believing in Him, I can be a part of Your family.*

**DIGGING DEEPER:**  God chose a group of people, the Jews, to be a special nation, Israel. Gentiles were outside the covenants of Israel, without God and without hope. The whole olive tree represents the family of God, with the root being the Jews under God's original covenant. The rest of the olive tree represents everyone who believes in Jesus and has been grafted in because of their faith. Galatians 3:28 says, "There is neither Jew nor Greek, . . . for you are all one in Christ Jesus."

**OVER THE GARDEN FENCE:** When grafting a fruit tree or rose, use a clean, razor-sharp edge to minimize damage to plant cells and encourage quick healing.

# 28

# CRACKED POTS

*He heals the brokenhearted and binds up their wounds.*
**(Psalm 147:3)**

One of my favorite plants is a perennial called creeping jenny. A few years ago, I put this plant in one of my terra cotta pots, and by summer, it had filled the container and was cascading over the sides, resembling a blanket of green fabric.

The sun would often find me sitting on my front porch watching the day begin. Looking over at the plant one morning, I saw a crack at the top of the pot, along the rim under the lush green leaves. The thought of disturbing my established plant was not an option. I tended to my creeping jenny and the cracked rim of its home all summer, giving the pot special attention as I watered, being careful not to cause more damage. It was broken, but I still had use of it and kept it close to protect it.

Our Master Gardener does the same with us—the brokenhearted. Who are we? We're people who've been crushed, disappointed, and hurt. We've experienced deep emotional pain caused by others, by circumstances, or by ourselves. He sees our cracks, but He still has use of us. Do you remember a time your heart was broken or when you were disappointed, grieving, hurting, or crushed? It could've been something you did or something that happened to you. Maybe it was circumstances beyond your control that caused you pain. Perhaps you're one of the brokenhearted at this very moment. Let me encourage you, the Master Gardener holds you close and keeps you near Him. He even sent His son, Jesus Christ, to heal your broken heart.

**PRAYER:** *Lord, I'm thankful You see past my brokenness and You still have a use for me. Help me to rest in this thought today—that I'm under Your care.*

**DIGGING DEEPER:** I think we have all, at one time or another, felt broken like a cracked pot. But I want to speak God's truth from the Bible into those places of brokenness. God sees you (1 Peter 3:12), God hears you (Psalm 18:6), and God knows you (Psalm 139:1, 23).

**OVER THE GARDEN FENCE:** Since it's difficult for a gardener to throw anything away, I've found a use for the broken pieces of clay pots. I place small sections of the broken pot at the bottom of larger containers so the water will drain down and away from the roots, which prevents them from staying too wet.

# 29

# HONEYBEES

*How sweet are your words to my taste, sweeter than honey to my mouth!*
**(Psalm 119:103)**

A garden can be a solitary, quiet place, and for some of us, the quietness is what we're looking for when we're outside. A spot where the silence rides the breeze in a delightful way that soothes, encourages, and relaxes. But looking closer, we can see we aren't alone. Often, I've taken a book outside to read only to find I'm sharing my space with honeybees, bumblebees, dragonflies, and butterflies. The antics of their flight keep me entertained until I stop to think of the seriousness of their jobs, especially the honeybees, which are to pollinate and make honey. Honey offers many health benefits because it's a good source of energy, rich in vitamins and minerals, and it tastes wonderful.

The psalmist who penned the above scripture refers to God's Word as sweet to the taste, sweeter than honey. Honey, that natural substance, for which bees give their life to sustain ours. Sound familiar? The Master Gardener gave His Son to come to this earth and die for us. The Bible is full of words that are sweeter than honey, life-sustaining words that allow us to know the heart of God, the sacrifice of His Son, Jesus, and the power of the Holy Spirit.

Carve out time today and find a quiet place to read the words that are sweeter than honey.

**PRAYER:** *Lord, may the honeybees be a constant reminder of the sweet and life-staining words found in the Bible.*

**DIGGING DEEPER:**  I have a friend who eats a spoonful of honey daily. He says it has many health benefits, and he'll go through the list. How much more beneficial is the Word of God for our spiritual well-being? Reading Scripture can transform us and deepen our relationship with God. If we think about it, most of the issues we face during the day aren't smooth or palatable, like honey, but rather the opposite. God's Word is unlike anything else. Read verses from the Psalms, and let God's Word nourish, encourage, and give you strength.

**OVER THE GARDEN FENCE:** Is your outside space small? No problem. Use containers to design areas of color and interest. You can even attract wildlife to your place by selecting plants that attract pollinators, butterflies, and hummingbirds. No area is too small for color and activity.

# 30

# DON'T COUNT ME OUT

*I formed you . . . you will not be forgotten by me.*

**(Isaiah 44:21)**

move often, and most of my plants move with me. I can't leave behind heirloom plants like my great-grandparents' irises or my grandmother's daylilies. How do I pack and move my plants? One way is to dig them up and drop them into plastic grocery bags. When I get to my new home, I take them out and plant them in the ground or in containers as soon as possible.

After one move in the fall, I discovered I'd missed a bag the following spring. As I lifted the bag, a clump of dirt fell to the ground, and in the middle of the clump I found a small, anemic daylily. To my surprise, it was trying to unfurl its stem and leaves to get through the soil and plastic bag toward the light. I could almost hear it saying, "Don't count me out!" I found a special place for this insistent plant, adamant to survive no matter the circumstances.

Looking at the struggling but determined plant, I saw myself, for I've been planted only to be dug up time after time and replanted. Like the daylily, I've gone through difficult circumstances where I felt left alone in a bag full of dirt, thrown away in the garden of life, and presumably forgotten. Oh, but I, too, shout, "Don't count me out!" For as small and anemic as I may feel, I continue to get through the circumstances and lean toward the light of my Master Gardener. I know I've not been forgotten and He still has a place for me to grow, bloom, thrive, and be used. And you've not been forgotten either.

**PRAYER:** *Lord, I'm thankful You formed me and You haven't forgotten me, even if I feel as though I've been tossed away.*

**DIGGING DEEPER:** Do you feel you've been replaced or everyone is moving onward and you're being left behind? It's not a good feeling. Stay strong and encouraged as you push through, like I found my anemic daylily pushing through the dirt and bag. As you do, you may even hear God cheering you on and shouting, "I haven't forgotten you!"

**OVER THE GARDEN FENCE:** Before you move plants, water them thoroughly a few days before packing. Make sure you place them in a sturdy container or in bags. For delicate plants, wrap in sheets or thin towels to protect foliage or blooms.

# 31

# WATER, WATER, WATER

*So neither he who plants nor he who waters is anything,*
*but only God who gives the growth.*
**(1 Corinthians 3:7)**

The number one killer of plants is not watering enough. The number two killer is overwatering. Here are some helpful tips for watering our houseplants and outdoor plants.

Check the soil moisture to determine how much water to add.

Know your plants and how much water they require.

Water deeply—don't throw a little water on a plant now and then and expect it to grow.

Understand that watering once isn't always enough.

We can use these same tips when we're sharing the message of Jesus Christ with others.

We must see how much the person we are ministering to already knows about Jesus and determine if they're ready to go to a deeper place in their relationship.

Knowing the person's background can help us know how much we need to water with God's Word.

We need to share beyond the surface, from our hearts, the words God gives us and, if possible, be a constant presence in that person's life.

Sharing our faith with someone once may not be enough. We may need to gain their friendship, trust, and respect before we can share God's love.

Most of all, we need to remember that God is the one who gives growth to a person. We may be the one who plants, or we may be the one who waters, but again, it's God who gives the growth.

**PRAYER:** *Father, help me to be faithful in sharing about Your Son, Jesus, and then allow You to give the increase.*

**DIGGING DEEPER:** We read in Matthew 28:18–19 that before Jesus ascended to heaven, He commanded His followers to make disciples, baptize them, and teach them. We all should be sharing the gospel.

**OVER THE GARDEN FENCE:** Check container moisture more often than ground moisture. This is important toward the end of the summer when the roots of our plants have almost filled the container and the soil is limited. If dry, water well, and then water again.

# 32

# TIME WITH THE MASTER GARDENER

*Seek the LORD and his strength; seek his presence continually!*
**(1 Chronicles 16:11)**

I enjoy spending time outside. If I'm not planting, I can often be found cultivating the soil, pruning, and fertilizing in my flower beds, for these are necessary tasks. The same can be said about reading and studying God's Word. I take time to sit and learn from the Master Gardener.

During these special moments with Him, I read His Word and prepare to grow. It's the same as cultivating my soil to prepare for growing plants; I cultivate my heart for growth in my spiritual life as I read the Bible and apply it to my life.

Pruning isn't fun, but it's essential. I must allow the Holy Spirit to remove sinful behaviors and negative attitudes that keep me from growing strong. Pruning also encourages new growth and prepares me to be more Christ-like.

For my plants to grow strong and healthy, they need nutrients, and the same goes for me. I can't expect to stay strong and grow in my walk with the Lord if I don't read His Word. It's during these moments that I begin to develop a deeper relationship with Jesus and begin to be more like Him. This makes me stronger to resist temptation, gives me wisdom, and increases my faith.

I've never spent time in my garden only to later walk into the house regretting it, and it's the same with the Master Gardener. Never have I walked away from reading, studying, meditating, and praying that I felt I'd wasted my time. Never. Being outside rejuvenates me, as does being with the one who loves me, cares for me, provides for me, and will never leave me.

**PRAYER:** *Lord, help me to make time to spend with You, seek You, and gain strength from You.*

**DIGGING DEEPER:** "But seek first the kingdom of God and his righteousness, and all these things will be added to you" (Matthew 6:33). We can have other interests, hobbies, and activities, but we must make sure we seek God first.

**OVER THE GARDEN FENCE:** When designing a garden, plan for many months of color. Select plants that will bloom early as well as midyear and late in the year. Even add items for winter interest by choosing plants that produce berries or have a unique form. Design your own personal sanctuary to enjoy.

# 33

# STEADY AS YOU GO

*"Be steadfast, immovable, always abounding in the work of the Lord,
knowing that in the Lord your labor is not in vain."*
**(1 Corinthians 15:58)**

"The hum of bees is the voice of the garden," according to Elizabeth Lawrence. In the quietness of the garden, one can hear the low hum of the bumblebees as they move from plant to plant. These steady workers could go unnoticed if not for their round bodies covered in soft black and yellow fur. Sometimes they can be covered with pollen as they push deep into the flower, gathering nectar and transferring pollen.

They're hard workers, and their bodies were designed to do the work the Master Gardener created them to do. From the tiny hairs that catch and carry pollen, their large size that allows them to pollinate a large variety of plants, to the soft hum that helps them to perform buzz pollination, they move with purpose. They're dedicated and spend their entire lives performing the job for which they were created.

The Master Gardener has created us, given us abilities and gifts, and like bumblebees, we, too, should move with purpose. We should stay focused and busy telling others about Jesus and the hope we have in Him. As Paul told the church in Corinth, we should be steadfast, dedicated as we labor. If we stay busy as bees, which many of us do, may we be busy about the work of the Lord, for our work will not be in vain.

**PRAYER:** *Lord, I pray You will help me serve You faithfully as I use the gifts and abilities You've given me.*

**DIGGING DEEPER:** Have you heard of the Pareto principle, also known as the 80/20 rule? Churches use this principle to suggest that 20 percent of the people do most of the work, while 80 percent remain less involved. We should be busy not for busyness' sake but for the sake of the Lord. If you're serving, may the Lord continue to bless your efforts. If you aren't, begin to ask Him what you can do in your local church or community using the gifts and abilities He has given you for such a time as this.

**OVER THE GARDEN FENCE:** We can protect bees by avoiding insecticides on plants, especially when they're in bloom. Remember to choose a variety of native flowering plants and to provide undisturbed areas for a safe place.

# 34

# GARDEN LIGHT

*You are the light of the world.*
**(Matthew 5:14)**

Do you have light fixtures in your garden? If used correctly, they can transform your outdoor space. I've seen people use solar lamps for pathways, twinkle lights in trees for ambience, lanterns to illuminate a seating or dining area, spotlights to highlight special trees, and spheres to illuminate around pools and on lawns.

The best lighting is a mix. Incorporate a soft glow for a cozy feel or bright functional beams for steps and paths. Design spaces in your yard as rooms and light them accordingly. And don't forget to place lanterns among your plants, for drama and decoration. Be creative by adding a touch of whimsy among your plants, a splash of color among your shrubs, or a lamppost near a bench.

Light is welcoming, and people are drawn to it. Our Master Gardener knows this, and He wants us to be a light in this world. In Matthew 5:16, we read, "Let your light shine before others, so that they may see your good works and give glory to your Father who is in heaven." Are we shining our light in a dark world? Do we shine brightly so people are drawn to us? We should think about this throughout our day. We, as gardeners, can begin to have tunnel vision as we keep our heads down working and tending, sowing and reaping, watering and feeding. We can do the same in our daily lives, but it shouldn't keep us from shining the light God has placed inside us.

**PRAYER:** *Lord, in my busy life, help me to remember to shine the light You have placed in me.*

**DIGGING DEEPER:**  It's easy to get complacent as we go about our daily routines. We lose sight of the great truth that we are to be a light in this world, like Jesus. God has called us to be more like His Son. How? We must learn all we can about Him so we can be like Him.

**OVER THE GARDEN FENCE:** What lights are best for you? Decide how you want to use the area in your landscape or garden. Do you need bright lights for safety or low lights for ambience? Their function will help you decide and give you guidance.

# 35

# HIS WONDROUS WORKS



*Tell of all his wondrous works!*
**(1 Chronicles 16:9)**

What's your favorite flower? One of mine is sunflowers—sunshine atop strong green stems looking up toward the sun.

I've always admired these beautiful flowers from the front, but once I glanced at them from behind, I was amazed. They looked like two different plants! Gone is the cheerful face full of seeds that feed an abundance of birds, as well as being my husband's favorite snack on the golf course. Gone are the fans of yellow ray florets surrounding the center. Viewing from the back, I see the green overlapping brackets, which serve as a protective layer for the flower as it begins to bloom. Such an interesting, scalloped pattern it creates around the base of the flower. How have I missed this? It's beautiful. And I want to talk about it!

We can get caught up in the ordinary—the familiar—and overlook the wondrous works from the Creator of the universe, the Master Gardener. Are you taking time to look around and see the wonderment of God? Are you searching beyond the familiar? When you do, are you acknowledging His creation? I've found this can be one of the easiest ways for me to tell others about Jesus, the Creator of the universe, in a way that's as nonthreatening as a dragonfly landing on my autumn sedum. Try it, let your garden be your conversation starter, and give others a new outlook of our wonderful Savior. He's beautiful and so is His creation, and we should always want to talk about Him!

**PRAYER:** *Lord, as I look around and see Your wondrous works, give me courage to share about You and all You've created.*

**DIGGING DEEPER:** We love our flowers and our plants that we've nurtured in our gardens. However, do we use our hobby, our love for gardening, to share Christ? Next time you talk to a friend about a new plant or an idea for your yard, ask God to show you how you can also share about Him.

**OVER THE GARDEN FENCE:** Want to grow your own sunflowers? Plant seeds after the last frost, about one to two inches deep and six inches apart. Plant them in plenty of sunlight, at least six to eight hours per day, and make sure you water often. Stake tall varieties to protect from wind damage.

# 36

# MY GARDEN BANNER

*The LORD Is My Banner.*

**(Exodus 17:15)**

When I'm in the garden, the wind is not my friend. Let me take that back—if it's a warm breeze cooling me while working on a hot day or causing my wind chimes to sing, I'm all for it. A sturdy gust I can do without because it can cause damage to my plants as well as other items in my yard, porch, and garden.

The enemy of our souls can be as damaging as wind—he wants to come into our lives and bring about as much chaos as possible. We can't see him the same way we can't see wind, but the evidence of him is there as he attempts to leave destruction in his wake. If we keep a watchful eye over our gardens, how much more does our Master Gardener keep a watchful eye over us?

Even though we do have an enemy, one that schemes against us, we also have one whose name is Yahweh Nissi, "The Lord Is My Banner," and it's a name that proclaims His protection over us (Exodus 17:15).

We all feel we are in a battle at one time or another, and we can feel alone. When these times come, remember Yahweh Nissi is watching over you, protecting you, and under His watchful eye, you are safe in His loving care.

**PRAYER:** *Thank you, Lord, that I'm never alone and that You're always protecting my family and me.*

**DIGGING DEEPER:** The name Nissi describes a flag or banner. In this instance, it points to the idea that God is victorious in battle and His flag is lifted high. When in battle, the Israelites would follow the banner, the leadership of God, as He led them and protected them. We, too, can walk under God's banner of protection. When things get difficult, remember God is victorious in battles, even if we don't see the evidence today. He is fighting our spiritual battles now, and He is faithful to give us strength to endure.

**OVER THE GARDEN FENCE:** A good way to protect plants from disease is to make sure all tools are clean before using them. Also, keep debris to a minimum and water at the base of the plant, not on the leaves. Select disease-resistant varieties whenever possible, and use the recommended plant spacing.

# 37

# WEEKLY FEEDING

*Like newborn infants, long for the pure spiritual milk, that by it you may grow.*
**(1 Peter 2:2)**

Having worked for years at a local garden center, I know the secret behind all those beautiful and lush plants that are on display. Are you ready for it? Fertilizer. Twice a week. No matter what. We had a fertilizing schedule, and you could mark the days of the week by these feedings. Often, our customers would come back a few weeks after purchasing plants and start asking why their plants weren't doing well.

"Are you feeding them?"

It's the first question we'd ask because sometimes a novice gardener assumes they only need to put the new plants in the ground or in a container, add water, and they will flourish as ours did. They had yet to learn that for plants to grow and perform successfully, they need proper nourishment or they will stay small and weak.

Our Master Gardener must want to ask us the same question when we go to Him in prayer about an issue in our lives. He knows if we aren't spending time in His Word learning and maturing, we won't grow strong and will stay weak. We need to be reading the Bible daily, feeding the spiritual part of us as we feed the physical part. If we don't eat, we will become weak, and it's the same with our spirit. We need to feed on God's Word so we may grow stronger.

**PRAYER:** *Lord, help me to be more faithful in reading Your Word and spending time with You so I can grow stronger spiritually.*

**DIGGING DEEPER:** How much time do you spend reading the Bible? Do you have a plan? If not, let today be the day you start reading and studying. Timothy teaches us we should do our best "to present yourself to God as one approved, a worker who has no need to be ashamed, rightly handling the word of truth" (2 Timothy 2:15).

**OVER THE GARDEN FENCE:** I use two types of fertilizer: slow-release and water-soluble. I use the slow-release on my trees, shrubs, and perennials, and the water-soluble on my annuals. To most people, it's a personal preference. Try both and see which one works best for you and your schedule.

# 38

# THE GARDEN PATH

*You make known to me the path of life.*
**(Psalm 16:11)**

Do you enjoy visiting different gardens? I do, whether it's a large botanical garden, a small, intimate one in my area, or at a friend's house. I appreciate seeing what others have created, and the more paths there are, the more enjoyable it is for me.

Garden paths are essential because they provide access to areas, define spaces, and entice movement while guiding visitors. They can provide amusement and mystery if designed to meander and weave around and through the landscape. Who doesn't appreciate taking a footpath leading to a garden gate covered with an arbor of fragrant jasmine or honeysuckle vine, inviting hummingbirds to feed.

86

If only the paths in life were as enchanting and delightful as a garden path. The ones we walk on as we go through life are filled with joy, fear, hurts, laughter, and tears. We place one foot in front of the other, not knowing where we're being led, what's around the bend, or who we'll bump into along the way. Can you relate? It may be fun to wait and see what's around the corner, but it can also be frightening. It's at these times that the Master Gardener shows up along the way to walk with us and be our guide. He's there during all the joy, fear, hurts, laughter, and tears. He doesn't want us traveling alone. He wants us to trust Him as we navigate the twists and turns, the ups and downs, the dark places, as well as the bright sunny spots of our journeys.

**PRAYER:** *Lord, I thank You for walking through this life with me and showing me the direction in which I should go.*

**DIGGING DEEPER:** The Bible teaches in Matthew 7:13–14 about two gates that lead to two paths. One is a narrow gate that leads to a path of everlasting life, and few find it. The other gate is as wide as the path and leads to destruction, and many go in by it. Which path have you taken? How you answer will determine where you'll spend eternity.

**OVER THE GARDEN FENCE:** When designing a garden, consider implementing paths to guide your guests and define spaces. Choose the material that best suits your budget and the look you want to achieve.

# 39

# OLD FRUIT

*They still bear fruit in old age.*

**(Psalm 92:14)**

"This will be a perfect addition to my garden," I thought to myself as I brushed the leaves and farming soil off the rusty treasure I'd discovered. What a surprise to find an old gate to a fence on my grandparents' farm that had been discarded and forgotten. I couldn't wait to see a morning glory vine gracefully growing on it, as well as have a special piece of my family's past in my garden.

Running up the familiar brick steps and into the back door, I eased around my granddaddy's walker, sat beside him, and asked for the old garden gate, only to be told no. The answer he gave surprised me, but the reason he gave will forever be in my mind.

"Well, Beth, I don't know, I may want to use it."

Here sat my granddaddy, an old man in his late eighties, using a walker to get around and still thinking of a way he could use that gate. I think of this often when I feel I'm too old to start a new garden project. I think the same in my spiritual life. Sometimes I feel too old to teach a Bible study, mentor a new Christian, or serve at my church.

The Master Gardener wants us to be productive, and age doesn't matter. Even as we grow older, we can and should be producing fruit and making a difference in others' lives as we point them to Jesus. After my granddaddy's passing, I got his gate, and it's the perfect addition to my garden and a reminder that I'm never too old to be used by God.

**PRAYER:** *Thank you, Lord, for the assurance that as I age, You still have a purpose for me to bear fruit for Your kingdom.*

**DIGGING DEEPER:** Even though the joints may ache and our energy level isn't what it used to be, God still wants us to bear fruit in old age. Colossians 1:10 encourages us "to walk in a manner worthy of the Lord, fully pleasing to him: bearing fruit in every good work and increasing in the knowledge of God." The more we learn about God, the more we will want to bear fruit and please Him, no matter what our age.

**OVER THE GARDEN FENCE:** Choose vines wisely. Just because you saw one growing along the roadside doesn't mean it's right for your yard. Many native vines are vigorous and invasive, so select varieties that are easy to grow and maintain.

# 40

# ROCKS AND MORE ROCKS

*I can do all things through him who strengthens me.*
**(Philippians 4:13)**

A new flower bed—another dream for my ever-evolving backyard. I couldn't wait to get started, and fall couldn't get here soon enough.

Gathering my shovel and wheelbarrow on a cool day, I began making my dream come true. After scraping off the top layer of grass and dumping it into the wheelbarrow, I took it to the back of the property and dumped it beside the fence. Then I returned to my chosen spot, and the digging began. All was well until I hit a rock. I worked it out, threw it into the wheelbarrow, and continued. Then I hit another rock, and then another, and another. My dream of a beautiful flower bed began to fade with each rock I uncovered.

This can happen to us when we have creative ideas we believe the Lord has put in our hearts to serve Him. We get excited, begin working, and then we hit the rocks of life, those unforeseen circumstances that prevent us from reaching our goal. Sometimes we must do some heavy lifting spiritually to get those obstacles out of the way of what God has for us to do. I had to move the rocks out of my backyard by myself, at least until I began incorporating them into the garden. But when we hit the hard places in life, we don't have to worry about all the heavy lifting, because the Master Gardener gives us the strength we need.

Let's keep dreaming, digging, and working. God will give us the strength because we can do all things, the easy and the difficult, through Christ who strengthens us.

**PRAYER:** *Lord, sometimes I get tired of moving obstacles out of my way. I'm so thankful that You're always with me and that You give me strength when I need it.*

**DIGGING DEEPER:** What obstacles are you facing, or what burdens are you carrying today? Think of these and then take a deep breath and focus on the truth that's in today's scripture. It's not only words but a promise that God gives us the strength we need through Christ Jesus.

**OVER THE GARDEN FENCE:** Don't throw all the rocks away. Look them over for interesting textures, colors, or marks to use as focal points in your garden, borders, water features, and rock gardens.

# 41

# IT'S NOT ABOUT YOU

*Let no one seek his own good, but the good of his neighbor.*
**(1 Corinthians 10:24)**

To cut or not to cut. That's a question I get when it comes to deadheading coneflowers. Yes, you may cut the flowers, and the plant will produce more blooms during the summer. However, later in the summer, I stop deadheading. The area may begin to look untidy, but in this instance, it's no longer about me—it's about my birds. The seedheads provide food for birds well into the winter and provide a home for beneficial insects.

Often, we make decisions based on what we like, need, or want. But as we read in 1 Corinthians, we need to seek the well-being of others before our own. It's not always about us in our daily lives. We think only toddlers scream, "Mine!" but we often do the same as adults. Our flesh nature leads us to look out for ourselves, but the Master Gardener wants us to emulate Jesus and put others first.

Keep this scripture close to you. Be the person who makes someone else's day better. We never know what another person is going through at any given time. Remember, it's not about you or me but others' well-being.

**PRAYER:** *Father, bring people in my path today to whom I can be a blessing. Help me to take my eyes off myself and meet another person's need.*

**DIGGING DEEPER:** We all seem to be busy. I think the busier I am, the more selfish I become. Not that I plan it that way, but it's easier to think about myself than others when short on time and energy. Do you remember the last time someone did a thoughtful deed for you and put you first? How did that make you feel? Return the gesture today. You will be the one blessed.

**OVER THE GARDEN FENCE:** You may already be leaving spent flowers and twigs behind for your birds and insects in your garden, but if not, try it this year. And if you live in an area that has snow in the winter, you will be pleasantly surprised by the visual interest you will receive from not cutting back all your perennials. Get your camera out. You don't want to miss the winter displays.

# 42

# LATE BLOOMERS

*Humble yourselves, therefore, under the mighty hand of God so that at the proper time he may exalt you.*

**(1 Peter 5:6)**

"Where did you take this picture?" I asked my brother as I looked at his beautiful photograph of acres of sunflowers at sunset. The colors were amazing, and all the flowers were standing tall as if to say good-bye to another day. I knew I had to take my own pictures, but with my schedule, I'd need to wait a few days . . . well, more like a week.

Making the hour-long trip later than I'd planned, I followed his directions and soon found the field he'd photographed. But wait! It couldn't be the same place. All those magnificent sunflowers in his picture were now facing the ground. I was too late. The seeds had matured and become heavy, causing the flowers to droop. And then I saw them: a few flowers standing tall as if they were greeting me. They were late bloomers, and even though few, they were magnificent.

Have you ever felt like a late bloomer? Always a little behind everyone else in your circle of friends, career, or family? It's okay. Those few amazing sunflowers I saw that evening rising above the others were as beautiful as the plants that had just passed their prime. The Master Gardener does the same in our lives. He will exalt us if we humble ourselves, trust Him, and wait for His timing. And guess which plants had my full attention at that moment? Not the masses past their peak but the late bloomers. And they were beautiful. If you are a late bloomer, you are beautiful too!

**PRAYER:** *Lord, that I would humble myself to Your ways and timing. You are the one who can and will exalt me. Give me patience until then.*

**DIGGING DEEPER:** How many times have you watched others advance in their career, get married, have babies, and some retire while you are waiting for your turn? It happens. We can get caught up in other people's lives and lose sight of the one who has the best plan for us. Ask the Lord to give you patience and help you focus on Him.

**OVER THE GARDEN FENCE:** If you have bird feeders and use sunflower seeds, don't pull the seedlings up when they sprout below the feeder. It may not look neat, but if you let them grow, you will be rewarded with new flowers. You and your birds will enjoy them.

# 43

# AFTER THE RAIN

*He will come to us as the showers, as the spring rains that water the earth.*
**(Hosea 6:3)**

John Updike claimed, "Rain is grace; rain is the sky descending to the earth; without rain, there would be no life." I love a good rain shower—preferably a gentle rain rather than what we in the South call a gully washer. The gentle showers allow the water to soak into the ground, unlike hard showers, which tend to run off rather than penetrate the soil. Without water, the ground will become dry, roots won't be able to get the water they need, and the plants will eventually die.

We can get dry spiritually. During this time, we feel as though our prayers aren't being heard, and our joy gradually fades like a delicate orchid flower hanging onto the stem, waiting for the other flowers to wither. It can be a slow process that drains our energy to the point we need reviving.

What a blessing it is to receive an encouraging word from someone as unexpected and needed as a rain shower. That's what the Master Gardener does: He orchestrates encouragement, joy, and refreshment through a friend, a meaningful worship service, or His written Word, to refresh us and help us grow. Next time you sit at your window and watch a gentle rain, afterward remember God comes to us like rain to encourage our faith.

**PRAYER:** *Lord, help me to be an encouragement to others during their storms.*

**DIGGING DEEPER:**  Want to be a better encourager? Here are five tips: 1) Listen to others. 2) Be gracious and don't judge. 3) Text while a person is on your mind before you forget. 4) Send a handwritten note or card. 5) Offer a good hug . . . nothing encourages more than a hug that shows you care.

**OVER THE GARDEN FENCE:** Rain gauges help measure precipitation levels. From simple ones to fancy and complicated, you'll find many to choose from. Place at least two to five feet off the ground in an open space, away from trees or buildings. Also, keep away from sprinklers, and place on a level surface or post for accurate readings.

# 44

# DEADHEADING

*Let us also lay aside every weight, and sin which clings so closely.*
**(Hebrews 12:1)**

"Why do I need to cut the old flowers off my plants? Can't I just let them stay?"
It's a question we often get from new customers at the garden center who want flowers but don't want to spend time caring for them. I understand not all of us relish getting dirty, fighting bugs, or the heat, and would rather look out our windows and gaze at the colorful display. But if we want more flowers, we need to remove the old ones when they die.

The reason we remove the dying flowers is that if we don't, they'll produce seeds, and the plant will think it's nearing the end of life and prepare to die or go dormant. By cutting the dead flowers before seeds are produced, the plant will continue to produce more flower buds.

Likewise, sometimes we need to remove sins and habits from our lives before they bring us to the point of death or dormancy. The Master Gardener requires this of us if we are to continue growing and being used by Him. It's not easy, and it's not fun. But we can't sit in front of the windows of our lives and expect God to bless us and allow us to flourish when we don't get rid of the sin that entraps us. It may be a dirty job, and we may get hot under the pressure, but the continuing beauty that comes is worth the effort.

**PRAYER:** *Lord, show me the sins and habits in my life that need to be removed so You can continue to use me.*

**DIGGING DEEPER:** The above scripture is often associated with running a race, but getting to the finish line is essential; so is continuing to grow and being used by the Lord. What is weighing you down? What sin traps you and keeps you from being used by God or allows the enemy to condemn you in your daily walk? Ask God to show you. He will, and He will guide you and love you through the process.

**OVER THE GARDEN FENCE:** Deadheading is a technique that removes spent flowers from a plant to encourage new blooms and keep it looking tidy. Pinch or cut the flower off below the dead flower and above the first set of full leaves. Exception with roses: Cut the stem above the fifth leaflet.

# 45

# SHARING

*The grass withers, the flower fades, but the word of our God will stand forever.*
**(Isaiah 40:8)**

I think gardeners are some of the most generous people. We enjoy sharing our knowledge, our seeds, and our plants. I've been the recipient of seeds, bulbs, plants, and tips along the way, which I always welcome. Then there are people like my friend who loves growing zinnias and other flowers to give as gifts. She works tirelessly, caring for her plants so they produce the most beautiful blooms to cut and give away. I have received some from her, and I must admit that nothing shouts "happy" like a mason jar full of colorful zinnia and sunflowers.

When I was younger, our church would invite men from Gideons International to speak, making us aware of the Bibles they shared around the world and raising money for future Bibles. Maybe you've seen one in a drawer of a hotel room or one resting on a table beside you in a hospital waiting room as you watched the clock while a loved one was in surgery. I know of others who raise money to have Bibles sent to China and other countries. I've also had friends tell me God prompted them to give away their treasured, well-marked Bible to someone they were witnessing to—a great sacrifice, but one they were happy to make for the Lord.

If gardeners are generous, how much more should Christians be when it comes to sharing God's Word, for as Isaiah reminds us, flowers fade, but the Word of God lasts forever. And nothing shouts "love" like the words from our heavenly Father.

**PRAYER:** *Lord, give me opportunities to share a Bible, God's Word, with others, either personally or through other organizations to reach the world for Christ.*

**DIGGING DEEPER:** Billy Graham said, "God has given us two hands—one to receive with and the other to give with. We are not cisterns made for hoarding; we are channels made for sharing." How true this statement is from one of the most well-known evangelists of our time. May we all pray for opportunities to be channels through which God's Word is shared.

**OVER THE GARDEN FENCE:** The best time to divide plants and share is in the spring or fall, but I've been known to divide them any time of the year. Whether using an old kitchen knife for small plants or my father-in-law's sawtooth handsaw, I make sure to cut through the root ball and replant sections with good growth and healthy roots.

# 46

# CREATED FOR A PURPOSE



*For by him all things were created, in heaven and on earth . . .*
*all things were created through him and for him.*

**(Colossians 1:16)**

Often, when I'm outside, the smallest flower will catch my attention. As I move closer, I can see the beautiful details of its petals, the shape of the tiny leaves, and the uniqueness that's contained in such a small treasure, and I'm delighted. But if I don't take the time to stop and notice, it's easy to miss the significance of the miniature charmer among all the bigger, showy plants.

Have you ever felt insignificant? I think we all have, and it's not a good feeling. We look around, and it seems others are living life to the fullest, receiving attention and accolades, while we move through our daily lives under the radar. But that's not how the Master Gardener sees us as He looks over His garden and His children. God finds delight in each of us, and we need to remember He created us through Jesus and for Jesus. He also has a plan for us, and in His economy it's not about how much money we make or how many honors and awards we receive, but about seeking after Him.

At some time or another, we all feel we're one of the small flowers that are being unnoticed, but God has His eye on us. He sees us in our busyness, pain, weakness, sorrow, and loneliness. Not only does He see us, but His Word also says in 2 Chronicles 16:9 (NLT), "The eyes of the Lord search the whole earth in order to strengthen those whose hearts are fully committed to him." What an encouragement to know God sees us, and He'll strengthen us if we commit ourselves to Him.

**PRAYER:** *Lord, help me to see that my significance is in You and You have created me special and for a purpose.*

**DIGGING DEEPER:** Are you, or someone you know, feeling insignificant at this moment? Take time today to recommit your life to God, seek His approval, not the approval of others, and ask Him to strengthen your faith. He sees you; He created you for a purpose, and He loves you. You are the delight of His heart.

**OVER THE GARDEN FENCE:** Want to make your garden and landscape more dramatic? Select plant material that offers a variety of sizes of flowers, leaves, and different shapes. What you see as insignificant can be a joy and be aesthetically pleasing to your visitors.

**47**

# DIGGING TO DANCING

*You have turned for me my mourning into dancing.*
**(Psalm 30:11)**

Knowing I was in the middle of writing my garden devotion book, one of my friends in my weekly writing group began sharing an idea with me about grief. She said, "Grief is like digging out a laurel hedge; it's more work than you expected, but once you're finished, you can plant something new, something beautiful." I realized she knew what she was talking about when she later told me that she'd experienced three miscarriages and became a widow at the age of thirty-eight. But she was right—something new has been planted and is growing in her life.

I understood her example of the laurel hedge. If you've ever looked over a section of your yard that has an established hedge, like laurel, and you want to remove it, you know the project sounds easier than it's going to be. The more you dig and pull up roots, the more roots you see, and the more you dig. It can be an overwhelming task, like grief. The more you dig and pull on the roots of grief, the more grief you find—but you keep digging.

After a time, a change happens. The one who loves us and says He will never leave or forsake us helps with our grief, and soon we're able to plant something new. My heart grieves as I write this, grief over the loss of someone I love, and even the grieving itself brings back other losses. Like the roots of the hedge, I thought I'd pulled it all up, but I find more grief. But the Master Gardener promises He will be with us in all things, and He will turn our mourning into dancing. Daily He plants joy in my heart, and yes, as I dig, I sometimes dance.

**PRAYER:** *Lord, what a comfort You are in my grief, and yes, in time You do turn our mourning into dancing.*

**DIGGING DEEPER:** "Jesus wept" (John 11:35). Yes, even Jesus felt grief and wept. He wept over his friend Lazarus, He wept for the city of Jerusalem, and He wept before He went to the cross. He felt great compassion then, and He does now. While we grieve, we can go to Him in our pain and hurt, and in time, He heals us. I look forward to heaven when Jesus "will wipe away every tear from their eyes, and death shall be no more, neither shall there be mourning, nor crying, nor pain anymore" (Revelation 21:4).

**OVER THE GARDEN FENCE:** We have different types of shovels for various tasks. A round-point shovel is suitable for digging and breaking soil, while a square-point shovel is ideal for scooping and moving loose material. My favorite? A round-point shovel with a short handle, because it makes it easier to dig holes in tight spaces, giving me better control.

# 48

# STILLNESS IN THE GARDEN

*Be still, and know that I am God.*

**(Psalm 46:10)**

When I design a garden, I try to create rooms. These rooms divide a yard into spaces that add interest and allow for places to stop and rest. As rooms in our homes need a chair, every garden needs a bench. The garden bench can be a place to relax, read, or enjoy the garden's tranquility.

The author of Psalms writes, "Be still, and know that I am God." I think of this scripture when I visualize the garden bench. It's a place where we can sit, meditate, and be still before the Master Gardener, for He is God and we are not. I need to be reminded of this many times throughout the week and sometimes daily.

The garden bench can also be a place to rest from our labors. The list of things to do while working outside can be long, and I often push myself too hard. I do the same in other areas of life too. Do you do the same? We need to know that we can stop and find rest from our labors and the trials of this life that concern us. The Master Gardener is waiting on us to be still before Him so He can give us rest and spend time with us. And if we sit quietly, we may hear Him singing over us (Zephaniah 3:17).

**PRAYER:** *Lord, draw me to the quiet places where I can be still and spend time with You.*

**DIGGING DEEPER:** The Hebrew word for the phrase "be still" is *rapha*, which means "to be weak, to let go, to release." We're not being called to inactivity but to stop striving and give control to God instead of hanging onto it ourselves. It's an invitation to give to Him all our cares and worries so we can rest in Him. What do you need to let go of today and let God have?

**OVER THE GARDEN FENCE:** Design an active garden, one that attracts wildlife. Enjoying time on a garden bench waiting for hummingbirds to arrive, butterflies to flutter, and bees to hum can be very relaxing.

# 49

# RUNAWAY GARDEN

*[Cast] all your anxieties on him, because he cares for you.*
**(1 Peter 5:7)**

Are you someone who appreciates a formal garden and is drawn to a more matchy-matchy, ordered look? Or are you one who finds joy in the loose, natural look of a native garden?

One is more difficult to maintain than the other because gardens don't play by the rules. If you want a formal garden, be ready to give it extra attention. If not, your morning glories will be running over your hydrangeas, and your primrose may end up across the border and become intertwined with your Shasta daisies. In other words, the garden will escape.

Isn't that the same as worry? We try to tame it, but if we don't stop worrying, it will escape and intertwine with our other emotions, such as joy and contentment, and eventually take over.

The Master Gardener wants to help us tame our worry and other emotions, including fear that can creep into our minds and our hearts. We read in 1 Peter that we are to cast all our cares upon Him. Why? Because He cares for us. He's constantly watching the worry as it moves across our hearts, and He is ready and waiting to help us contain it when it escapes. Give your cares to God, for they're not yours to carry. He's a big God, and He can handle them. We just need to let Him.

**PRAYER:** *Lord, help me to cast my cares upon You. And thank You for loving and caring for me.*

**DIGGING DEEPER:** Prayer is our most effective tool against worry. Paul writes to the Philippians, telling them not to be anxious about anything but to pray about every situation. God understands we're going to get caught up in our circumstances, but He offers an alternative to the ongoing and exhausting habit of worry. We're creatures of habit, and it's easy to fall back into worrying. How can we cast our cares upon Him? Start off our day with prayer, and pray throughout the day. Our heavenly Father understands our struggles, and He's ready to step in and take them from us.

**OVER THE GARDEN FENCE:** Need flowering climbers for a fence, wall, or gate? Here are a few of my favorites: jasmine, black-eyed Susan, passionflowers, fragrant honeysuckle, morning glories, and sweet peas.

# 50

# REPURPOSED



*Many are the plans in the mind of a man, but it is the purpose of the LORD that will stand.*

**(Proverbs 19:21)**

Repurpose. From barn doors to Aunt Lucy's mismatched silverware, if it's old and has no current purpose, it can be reused and given a new purpose. I've collected items for years to reuse. I've saved bricks from my parents' backyard, tools from my grandparents' farm, and old glass bottles my grandmother buried in her garden. (She always said glass would be replaced by plastic. Who knew? Well, she did!) One day, I hope to find a new use for each of these items, whether in my garden, kitchen, or garage. For now, they sit waiting.

Do you ever feel you're sitting, waiting to be reused—repurposed? Our Master Gardener has a design and plan for our lives as we do for our gardens and yards. He will take our experiences and knowledge and repurpose them for another assignment. He will take our brokenness, hurts, and past failures and transform them into a unique and beautiful purpose for His glory. It may be a new idea or project we've never considered, or He may promote us in our current role with new responsibilities.

What do we do now? We wait in a posture of prayer and seeking, and He will lead us to the next phase in our walk with Him. We keep our eyes focused on the Master Gardener because even though we may come up with our own plans, they may or may not flourish, but His plans for us will stand.

**PRAYER:** *Lord, help me to trust You and Your purpose for me and my life.*

**DIGGING DEEPER:**  I love the quote by Pastor Chuck Swindoll that says, "Stay open to surprises because they are a major part of God's leading—and He's full of them!" What we studied and trained for may not be what we end up spending the rest of our lives doing. God is in control, and if we're His, He's working things out for our good, and sometimes that may include being repurposed for His glory.

**OVER THE GARDEN FENCE:** What items can you repurpose? Look for items such as a copper pot and use it to store a garden hose. How about a galvanized tub or container to plant an herb or salad garden? Use a small watering can for pens, pencils, scissors, or other small tools. Have fun and be creative.

# 51

# MORNINGS IN THE GARDEN

*The steadfast love of the L*ORD *never ceases; his mercies never come to an end; they are new every morning.*
**(Lamentations 3:22–23)**

Getting up early in the morning to walk in the garden or sit on a porch, holding a warm cup of coffee while the morning dew glistens on the blades of grass and the petals of flowers, can be a special time. Being more of a night owl myself, I miss more of these moments than I want to admit. However, when I do get up early, I'm never disappointed by the morning light and the peacefulness it uncovers.

The author of the book of Lamentations tells us how special each day is by reminding us that our Master Gardener's compassion is new every morning. New, not old and used, but current. It's His love, mercy, and compassion that start as the sun rises and stay with us till nightfall.

Even if we wake up troubled—whether due to issues with our family, finances, health, or jobs—and feel hopeless, God is faithful. Not only does He see us, but we read in Lamentations 3:55–56 that He hears our voice.

Next time you're in your garden as the morning sun reaches out to touch His creation, or sitting by your window watching the light pass across the trees in your yard as the sun moves upward in the sky, ponder the new beginning, along with the new love, mercy, and compassion God has for you. Yes, He is faithful.

**PRAYER:** *Thank you, Lord, for Your love, mercy, and compassion for me—and the promise that they are new every morning.*

**DIGGING DEEPER:** Our journey through life can be challenging. Daily, we are beaten down and defeated, just as the people of Israel and Judah were. As Jeremiah encouraged them, he encourages us. God's mercies are not consumed—they never end. Each day we begin with new mercies, not leftovers from yesterday. Wake up knowing God's already waiting on you, whether you started early or late.

**OVER THE GARDEN FENCE:** Mornings are the best time to water plants. Watering at this time allows the water to be absorbed in the soil. The next best time is in the evenings. Avoid watering in the middle of the day if possible. But if you must, make sure you water at the base of the plants.

# 52

# THE LORD IS FAITHFUL

*But the LORD is faithful. He will establish you and guard you against the evil one.*
**(2 Thessalonians 3:3)**

A enjoy taking pictures in the rain, so when I get the chance, I'll venture out to photograph plants. After one such outing, I began looking through my photos when I returned home, and what a delight to see I'd captured a small bumblebee under the petal of a scented geranium seeking cover from the storm.

This reminded me of how the Master Gardener is faithful to guard us from the storms of life, as well as from people and situations that can harm us. The bee I caught on camera looked so cozy nestled under the petal of the flower as the rain fell. The flower didn't go to the bee, but the bee sought out the shelter of the flower. God will do His part, but we must be willing to go to Him in our time of need.

God wants us to feel safe. Just as the bee sought shelter, we, too, need to seek refuge and go to the one who is faithful and will strengthen and guard us. When life's troubles begin as a drizzle, we may not see the need for shelter or help, but then the storm or situation intensifies, and we start looking. God is near, waiting with a safe place for us.

**PRAYER:** *Thank you, Lord, that You are faithful to shelter and guard me during hardships and the storms of life.*

**DIGGING DEEPER:** I recently attended the funeral of a godly lady at my church, and her younger sister shared how her older sister had been her friend and protector all her life. Being a firstborn, I can't relate to this. But the Bible tells me I do have a protector, and He's strong and faithful. I never have to wonder if He'll get tired and let His guard down. Do you have the assurance that you have a protector? May the Lord give you evidence of His faithfulness as He guards you and your family daily.

**OVER THE GARDEN FENCE:** Rainwater is softer than tap water and free of pollutants; therefore, it's good to use on indoor plants—especially delicate plants like orchids. To collect rainwater, place a large bucket under gutter downspouts or use rain barrels. Melted snow is also good to use when available.

# 53

# JUST ASK

*Always [be] prepared to make a defense to anyone who asks you for a reason
for the hope that is in you.*

**(1 Peter 3:15)**

When people hear I'm a horticulturist, gardener, or designer, or worked in a nursery, they begin to ask questions. I don't mind, unless they ask about fruit, vegetables, or lawn grasses. My degree is in ornamental horticulture, and I can answer most questions about flowers, shrubs, ground covers, trees, soil, seeds, fertilizer, and plant care. If I'd known so many people would ask about their fig trees or their squash and tomato plants, I'd have at least taken one class in fruits and vegetables. And don't ask me about your lawn. I didn't enjoy my Turf Management class at all, so I tell people, grass isn't my thing unless it's an ornamental grass.

I enjoy being asked gardening questions, and if I don't know the answer, I'll find out. I also don't mind being asked questions about my faith. I love to share what I've learned by studying the Bible as well as my experiences with the Lord.

As a Christ follower, we should be ready to answer questions when others ask about our faith. We don't have to quote Scripture with chapter and verse or get into a deep theological discussion; all we need to do is tell our story of what the Lord means to us and how our lives have changed since accepting Christ as our Savior.

And remember, just as I do, if you don't know the answer, you can always find out. Just be ready and be approachable. The Master Gardener is already working in their heart; we need to be prepared when they ask.

**PRAYER:** *Lord, help me to be ready to share my faith and the hope I have in You at any time today.*

**DIGGING DEEPER:**  People want to hear our God stories. Take time to think of what God has done for you and your family. Write a few examples down, even practice saying them. As you prepare to be used, God will be preparing others to ask. We need to be ready to share about the hope that's inside us, the hope the Lord gives us.

**OVER THE GARDEN FENCE:** Want to learn more about gardening? Look for gardening groups on Facebook, Instagram, or in your community. It's fun to learn alongside others. And remember, don't be afraid to ask questions—gardeners love to share their knowledge as much as they love sharing their plants.

# 54

# A DIFFERENT PERSPECTIVE

*And we know that for those who love God all things work together for good,*
*for those who are called according to his purpose.*

**(Romans 8:28)**

When I'm out with my camera, I'll walk back and forth in opposite directions, keeping my eyes open for something I may have missed. I move around examining flowers, objects, and landscapes to find the best way to capture a photo. I'm sure I'm not the only photographer who would almost stand on their head to get a good shot.

Maybe I won't stand on my head to survey my garden, but I use the same technique with my notebook in my hand instead of my camera. I spend time thinking about the cooler months ahead when I may need, or want, to move plants around or correct a problem. No garden is perfect, and neither is life.

Our Master Gardener helps us change our perspective when we face problems in our lives. We can't keep problems away any more than we can keep weeds out of our flower beds, but we can choose how we want to respond to them. By trusting God in all things, we'll have the assurance that God will work all things out according to His purpose. He may not change our circumstances, but He will help us see them through His eyes and guide us through whatever we are facing.

Next time you encounter a problem, step back, walk around it, and look at it from another perspective. And if you look beside you, God is right with you.

**PRAYER:** *Lord, help me to see my problems from Your perspective and trust You in the outcome.*

**DIGGING DEEPER:** What are you facing today? Does it look too big for you to handle? Take a step back and ask God to give you His perspective. Paul reminds us to "set [our] minds on things that are above, not on things that are on earth" (Colossians 3:2). When we set our minds on things above, we can begin to see our situations from God's perspective and trust Him when He says He's working all things out for our good, according to His purpose.

**OVER THE GARDEN FENCE:** Garden journaling is a great way to review and track your garden's progress year to year. Jot down ideas, draw future bed layouts, or record the date of your first hummingbird sighting. The best way to learn is by experience, and keeping notes can be invaluable.

# 55

# KNEELING IN THE GARDEN

*Oh come, let us worship and bow down; let us kneel before the LORD, our Maker!*
**(Psalm 95:6)**

"Do you want some of Grandmother's daffodils? I dug them up when extending her patio and would rather give them to you than throw them away."

As any gardener would, I said yes, especially since they were from my grandmother's yard. A few days later, my cousin brought me about fifty daffodil bulbs, and when fall arrived, I prepared to plant them. In honor of my dad, I pulled out his old bulb planter, then reached for my knee pad, gathered the bulbs, went to my backyard, sank to my knees, and began digging. It would be worth every hole I dug to see those beautiful yellow flowers ushering in spring.

Ushering in spring. That makes me think about ushering in the Lord's presence during our Sunday worship services. How does planting daffodils make me think of worshipping the Lord? It's what I do to prepare for Sunday. In the manner I prepare for bulb planting, I prepare for spending time worshipping.

In honor of Jesus, I pull out my Bible where I've dug deep in God's Word during the week, I think about the times I've been on my knees praying, I gather all my worries, fears, and concerns, and bury them before the Lord as I give my cares to Him. In His presence, I want to worship and focus on Him, not me.

If we can kneel to plant bulbs to beautify our garden, we can spend time in a posture of kneeling before the Master Gardener—the one who made heaven and earth and all we grow out of it.

**PRAYER:** *Lord, help me to prepare for worship, remembering to give You honor and glory for all You do and who You are.*

**DIGGING DEEPER:** Oil and water can't coexist; we know that's true. Here's another truth: Worship of God and promotion of self can't coexist either. To truly worship almighty God, we need to remove ourselves from the scene. That's why preparation for worship is important. How do you prepare for worshipping the Lord on Sundays and during the week?

**OVER THE GARDEN FENCE:** Want your daffodils to look natural and not in a formal row? In the fall, grab a handful of bulbs and throw them in the area you want them to grow and bloom. Dig the holes where the bulbs land, and you will have a gorgeous naturalized daffodil garden in the spring.

# 56

# BOUNDARIES

*I placed the sand as the boundary for the sea, a perpetual barrier that it cannot pass;
though the waves toss, they cannot prevail; though they roar, they cannot pass over it.*

**(Jeremiah 5:22)**

What does the ocean have to do with gardening? In my mind, they go together because they're my favorite two places to take my camera and enjoy God's creation. For a year, I lived in the Lowcountry of South Carolina on the coast, and I must admit I didn't do much gardening, but I did enjoy photographing the beauty around me. My love of the Lowcountry tiptoes into my thoughts as I ponder boundaries.

In terms of gardening, boundaries make me think of picket fences, boxwoods, and short stone walls to separate yards and flower beds. These structures keep plant material in place, define spaces, and provide protection. Boundaries are essential in our lives too. We need to set mental and physical limits to protect ourselves. The hedges and borders in our gardens are there not to keep the plants from growing and blooming but to help them thrive.

Our Master Gardener, the same one who placed the sand and told the waves they could not pass over it, can help us set our own boundaries. Do you have trouble saying no? Do you find it challenging to stay away from unhealthy relationships? Do you feel as though you're always busy but not accomplishing anything for the Lord? Let the Master Gardener help you, for as He's the Master of the seas, He can be Master of our lives if we'll give Him the opportunity.

**PRAYER:** *Lord, what a comfort to know that as I try to set boundaries for myself, You're willing and able to help me.*

**DIGGING DEEPER:** Setting personal boundaries can be daunting, but we can look to Jesus as our example. He set limits for Himself by making sure He had time alone away from the crowds and time to pray to His Father. He spoke truth in love, said no to inappropriate behavior, and set personal priorities for Himself. He surrounded Himself with people He could trust, and He looked to His Father for all His needs. "Guard your heart above all else, for it determines the course of your life" (Proverbs 4:23 NLT).

**OVER THE GARDEN FENCE:** Boundaries in the garden help make maintenance easier, keep flower beds tidy, and prevent our lawns from encroaching on our flowers. Choose from a wide variety of materials, including blocks, bricks, steel edging, and hard-plastic commercial landscape edging.

# 57

# WEED OR WONDER

*You will recognize them by their fruits.*

**(Matthew 7:16)**

With the warm sun on my back, I searched for my faithful friends to emerge from their winter slumber in a flower bed. As I removed leaves and debris from the soil, I noticed a green sprout emerging near the base of my birdbath. I didn't remember planting anything there. Do I pull it up or leave it?

I left it because I didn't know if I'd found a weed or a wonder. Spring came, and roses began their faithful show of color, hydrangea flowers were in abundance, and the daylily buds were starting to swell. At the same time, the weed or wonder grew with great diligence. Spring gave way to summer, and I watched, aware of the phlox blooming, the green stalk with unrecognizable leaves grow higher and higher. And then fall came. I looked out over the garden where the oak hydrangea leaves were beginning their autumn splendor and noticed the buds. A few days later, I saw a hint of yellow, and then one sunny October day, the most beautiful yellow flowers burst forth. It turned out to be a wonder, not a weed. I didn't know this until I saw what it produced.

The Bible says there'll be people who come in sheep's clothing to deceive us and lead us astray. We need discernment to evaluate people by the fruit they produce. Is it good or bad? Are they a weed or a wonder? How do we know? We ask the Master Gardener for wisdom. As we look to Him, we'll have confidence that He's watching and protecting our hearts from deception.

**PRAYER:** *Lord, help me to seek Your discernment about whether someone is a good, trustworthy person or someone who is going to lead me astray.*

**DIGGING DEEPER:** We need to recognize people who want to deceive us. How do we do this? Look at their fruit; in other words, listen to what they say, watch how they act, and notice the places they go. These will give us clues as to their character and their intent. We must be looking for those who speak truth and live out what God teaches in the Bible. If what we see or hear doesn't align with what's in the Bible, it's not of God and can harm us or lead us astray.

**OVER THE GARDEN FENCE:** To stake tall flowers, choose a sturdy stake and place it near the plant early in the growing season. Keep ties loose to allow for growth.

# 58

# REFLECTIONS OF GRACE

*For from his fullness we have all received, grace upon grace.*

**(John 1:16)**

A birdbath is a welcoming addition to any garden, but not just for the birds. As I move around my flower bed, I delight in seeing the different reflections in the water at various times of the year. From one angle, I can see the flowers on the fence behind the birdbath, and from another, I can watch the clouds on a summer day. Even in the fall, as I rake leaves, I can look over and see colorful leaves or petals resting on the water's surface.

When I'm out with my camera, I'm always looking for water—whether a puddle, a water fountain, a pond, or a lake. I'm able to capture the reflections they offer if I'm diligent in my seeking. Whether photographing the reflection of a bird flying over the waves at the shoreline or taking in the beauty of trees on an autumn day with their colors being brought to life as they're mirrored on the smooth surface of a pond, I'm looking.

Our Master Gardener is also seeking reflections. Even though He created the birds and the leaves that reflect in the water, He's more interested in what I'm reflecting. He wants me, and He wants you, to reflect His Son, Jesus, and His grace. How do we mirror Jesus? By spending time with Him through prayer, reading the Bible, and worship. If we call ourselves followers of Jesus, others should be able to see His reflection in us. We should love as He loves, forgive as He forgives, and extend grace as He extends grace.

**PRAYER:** *Lord, help me to know You better so I can reflect You and Your love to others.*

**DIGGING DEEPER:** We can mirror Jesus and His life in many ways. We must love as He loved, and He loved everyone, even His enemies. Jesus only did what the Father told Him to do, as we should. Are we being obedient in our daily lives? Spend time with the Lord in prayer today as you examine yourself and your actions, and ask God to make you more like Jesus.

**OVER THE GARDEN FENCE:** The best way to clean your birdbath is to empty the water, then scrub it with a brush to remove debris and algae. Use one part white vinegar to nine parts water for routine cleaning. Always rinse well and let dry before adding more water.

# 59

# THE WINTER GARDEN

*Even to your old age . . . I will carry you!*
**(Isaiah 46:4)**

Part of the enjoyment of gardening is seeing the work of our hands transformed throughout the year. In spring, we spend time cultivating, sowing, planting, and tending with some evidence of our labors in early-blooming bulbs and shrubs. Summer finds us busy watering, feeding, pruning, and reaping the benefits as we cut blooms for bouquets and watch pollinators and hummingbirds visit. With the coming of fall, the blooms begin to fade as the leaves become vibrant, and the cooler temperatures draw us out once again to survey the results of our toil. Then it's winter.

Winter in the garden can bring a stillness unlike any other time of the year. The ground becomes hard, and at times we wake to a veil of what looks like diamonds after an early-morning frost. Add snow, and the garden will take on different appearances as the snowflakes unite to cover plants and tree limbs, attaching themselves to the most insignificant objects, making them shimmer with a new beauty.

I think of winter as I ponder the different stages of life. I don't know which stage you're in, but winter seems to be the one people dread most. I can spend my short days and long nights remembering how much more I could do in my yard and long for those days of youth and strength, or I can do as my garden does. Rest. Yes, rest from the active growing season and be content. The Bible tells us even in our old age—our winter of life—God will be there to carry us.

**PRAYER:** *Lord, help me to remember You are with me in each season of my life and have a purpose for me, even as I rest.*

**DIGGING DEEPER:** Do you enjoy a time of rest, or do you fight it? Every growing season needs a season of rest, and as we continue to grow in our spiritual lives, we need it too. It's a holy pause for us to step back from striving, working, and proving. Whether you're in the winter of your life or your spiritual journey, remember to take time with the Lord to sit still and recharge.

**OVER THE GARDEN FENCE:** Add plants that'll bring interest in the winter, such as winterberry holly, red twig dogwood, and pyracantha, to name a few. Plant some early-blooming bulbs like snowdrops, and let the blooms of panicle hydrangeas catch the snow. For color, plant different varieties of camellias and don't forget pansies, violas, and snapdragons.

# 60

# CHANGES

*Jesus Christ is the same yesterday and today and forever.*
**(Hebrews 13:8)**

"I'll take one of these, a few of those over there, and oh, I have to have that one!"

That's me visiting my local nursery. I see new plants I've yet to grow, new varieties and colors I must have, and new projects I want to implement, and I like it all. I don't think I'm the only one who does this, because we gardeners can't pass up a new addition to our yard or garden.

Because of this fact, our gardens are ever-changing and constantly evolving. To me, that's what makes gardening enjoyable. I'm not an artist who gathers my heavy paper, paints, and brushes to create a work of art to place over my mantle, but my yard is my canvas as I design an outdoor masterpiece I can see from my windows. From season to season and through all my trial and error, it becomes my sanctuary.

As I watch spring tumble into summer, summer change to fall, and fall move into winter and then bounce back to spring, I'm aware my life does the same—it changes, sometimes for the good and sometimes for the not so good. But just as I can count on the sun rising each day, I know the Master Gardener will be with me through it all. My life may change and evolve, but He doesn't; He is "the same yesterday and today and forever." I need to be reminded of this truth at times. What about you? Do you feel you can't keep up with all that's going on, or when you try, life knocks you off balance? You're not alone. The fingerprints of love we read about in the Bible can be found in our lives, no matter the change. Take time to see the Master Gardener's fingerprints in every season of your life.

**PRAYER:** *Thank You, Lord, that You're the same no matter what changes come my way, and You walk me through them and give me the strength and guidance I need.*

**DIGGING DEEPER:** Change can be good, and the best change we can make in our lives is to accept Jesus Christ as our Savior and allow Him to make the ultimate change in us. The Bible says, "Therefore, if anyone is in Christ, he is a new creation. The old has passed away; behold, the new has come" (2 Corinthians 5:17).

**OVER THE GARDEN FENCE:** Janet Kilburn Phillips said, "There are no gardening mistakes, only experiments." Don't be afraid to make changes in your garden. Just as our lives change and evolve, so do our gardens. Enjoy the journey and the process.

# A NOTE FROM BETH

This garden devotion has been a blessing to write. However, I didn't anticipate that the words I was putting on paper would serve as a reminder of God's faithfulness to me as I walked through some of my own challenging moments. But through it all, the Master Gardener was always near.

He, the Master Gardener, is the reason for this book. And if you don't know Him, I would love to introduce you to Him. He's the God of the Bible. He was there at the beginning, the first garden, for we read in Genesis 1:1, "In the beginning God created . . ."

God created everything, and then He created man and woman to have fellowship with Him and be in His family. While they were living with God in the garden, the serpent (Satan) later came to Eve and tempted her, and she ate the fruit that God said was forbidden and gave some to Adam, and he ate it also.

They didn't immediately die physically, but they did spiritually. At that very moment, sin entered their lives. They lost the glory that surrounded them, saw they were naked, and tried to cover up with fig leaves. God had to sacrifice an animal to make them a covering of skin. He then banished them from the garden. God had to keep them from eating from the Tree of Life, because if they did, they would have lived forever in their sin.

When they died spiritually, they could no longer have fellowship or a relationship with God. Why? Because God is a holy God and He can't be in the presence of sin. When Adam and Eve sinned, fellowship was broken, and they could no longer be in the presence of their Creator, their heavenly Father. From Adam and Eve onward, every child has been and will continue to be born in sin. But God had a plan to redeem mankind. His plan was His own Son, Jesus.

Jesus came to bridge the gap between sinful man and a holy God. The wages of sin is death, and Jesus came to pay the sin debt for all of us. He died so we wouldn't have to. "For God so loved the world that He gave His only begotten Son, that whoever believes in Him should not perish but have everlasting life" (John 3:16 NKJV).

The Bible says that as soon as a person accepts that Jesus went to the cross, shed His blood, died for their sins, that He rose from the dead to defeat death forever, they are born again—born into God's family. Now they can be in a relationship with a holy God, through the blood of Jesus that He shed on the cross, and when they die, they'll live with Him for eternity.

In Day 3's devotion, "Container Gardening," I wrote about our citizenship in heaven, and this is the only way a person can live forever with the Master Gardener. In Day 38, "The Garden Path," I asked which path you've taken; one leads to eternal life and the other to everlasting destruction. And again, I ask, which path have you taken? Have you trusted Jesus for your salvation so you can live forever with the Master Gardener?

If you've never made this decision and are interested in accepting Jesus' gift of salvation, I wish I could sit on a garden bench and talk to you. I would share these verses and thoughts with you:

> "For all have sinned and fall short of the glory of God" (Romans 3:23).
> "For the wages of sin is death, but the free gift of God is eternal life in Christ Jesus our Lord"
> (Romans 6:23).

We have all sinned, which separates us from God, and there's only one way to be reconciled. It's by believing that His Son, Jesus, paid the penalty for our sin on the cross and bridged the gap between God and us. It's only through His death that our sin debt can be paid.

What's our response?

The Bible tells us, "If you confess with your mouth that Jesus is Lord and believe in your heart that God raised him from the dead, you will be saved" (Romans 10:9).

If you would like to receive Jesus Christ right now, this is how:

> Admit that you are a sinner and need a Savior.
> Be willing to repent (turn away) from your sins and ask for God's forgiveness.
> Believe that Jesus died for you on the cross and rose from the grave.
> Receive Jesus as Lord and Savior by praying and asking Him to come in and control your life through the Holy Spirit.

Here is a prayer you can pray:

> *Dear God, I admit that I'm a sinner and separated from You. I want to turn from my sins, and I ask Your forgiveness. I believe that Jesus is Your Son and that He died on the cross for my sins and that He rose from the grave. I don't want to be in control of my life anymore and want Jesus to come into my heart. I want to trust Jesus as my Savior and Lord and follow Him with my life. Thank you, Jesus, for saving me.*

Did you pray this prayer? I want you to know that God is in your midst; He does the saving. We also read in Zephaniah 3:17, "He will rejoice over you with gladness; he will quiet you by his love; he will exult over you with loud singing." What a beautiful picture of His love for you and for me.

If you prayed this prayer or have any questions, I would love to hear from you, for I have something I would like to send you to encourage you in your walk with Jesus.

Thank you for spending time with me at *The Potting Bench* as we learned from the Master Gardener. May these lessons stay with you beyond the garden, the same as mud on your shoes, dirt under your fingernails, and joy that's been cultivated in your heart.

And if these devotions have nourished your soul and drawn you closer to the Master Gardener, would you consider leaving a short review on Amazon, Barnes & Noble, Books-A-Million, Goodreads, and on your social media accounts? Your words may plant seeds of hope and encourage others who need a reminder of God's faithfulness.

**—Beth**

> "The Lord bless you and keep you; the Lord make his face to shine upon you and be gracious to you; the Lord lift up his countenance upon you and give you peace" (Numbers 6:24–26).

# ACKNOWLEDGMENTS

They say it takes a village to raise a child, but I found out it also takes a village to write a book. Yes, I'm the author, but I couldn't have done it without people who have helped me now and in the past. Vonda, I would never have stepped foot on the writing path without your encouragement. And Edie, for you both welcoming me as a newbie into your group and for teaching, mentoring, and cheering me on when I had no idea what it meant to be a writer and speaker. To you both, I'm forever thankful.

Cindy and Eddie, you accepted me into the Christian Devotions family as a new devotional writer, then as a contributor for *Inspire a Fire*, as part of the prayer ministry, and as faculty for ACWC, which started as Boot Camp one winter weekend in the North Carolina Mountains. Not only did you teach me how to write devotions, but you also showed me, by example, what a good work ethic looks like and how to seek God in all things as a writer and Christ follower.

LaTan, my longtime friend, you taught me to use what was in my hand. For the longest time, I didn't understand what that meant, but here it is—my teaching, love for God's Word, writing, speaking, horticulture degree, photography, and gardening experience in the pages of this book. May God receive all the glory from this work as I put it in His hands.

My Tuesday morning writers' group, you don't realize the courage and strength I gained from sitting around those long high-top tables with you as you worked on your own projects and books. Watching you write so faithfully made me want to be a better writer.

Michael, Larry, Jen, Geoff, Deb, and my Illumify family—what a learning experience this has been, and I'm thankful for each one of you and the many others who brought this project to fruition. Your knowledge, professionalism, creativity, and availability were impressive and most appreciated.

Jean, Kelli, Tammy, Cathy, Carol, Larry, Wendy, Sam—each of you has a part in this book. I will forever be grateful for the support, help, prayers, ideas, direction, and time you gave to me.

Barrett and Cindy, thank you for the house in Highlands for a weekend to write and for your encouragement.

Those I called and texted asking for prayer, you pounded the doors of heaven for me when I couldn't see my way to finishing this project. Thank you, Tammy, Kelli, Debbie, Debra, Dee Dee, Cathy, Wendy, Pastor Wayne, Ally, and Greg.

To my family, my Gospel Hour family, and my Cathedral Community Church family, you have cheered me on to the finish line and prayed for me every step of the way. Thank you.

Bob, my brother and photography buddy, thank you for your help with my photographs for this book and for encouraging me to step out and use them.

My sweet Mama, yes, you were the one who watched the seeds Daddy planted grow and mature. I wish he were here to see this book, but I know he's with the Master Gardener, and we will all be together again one day. Thank you for your love and support, and for always believing in me.

Ally, your constant love and encouragement keep me grounded. You're always there to listen, brainstorm, proofread, and talk me off the ledge when I need it. You are so dear to me, and you make me want to be a better person. I'm glad you were with me that afternoon at Summer Moon Coffee and were the one to see my tears when I finished this book. A moment I won't forget.

Greg, thank you for believing in me when I didn't believe in myself, for always supporting me and letting me be who God created me to be. You've been so gracious to let me sequester myself in my home office and local coffee shops to write, as well as spend a weekend in the mountains watching football games while I worked on this book. Not to mention how patient you always are when I wander off with my camera, taking pictures. I could not have accomplished this without you. I love you and appreciate you more than you will ever know.

Jesus, thank you for paying my sin debt on the cross so I can live in eternity with the Master Gardener, my heavenly Father. May You receive all the glory.

# ABOUT THE AUTHOR

Beth Fortune is a writer, speaker, photographer, and horticulturist with a degree in ornamental horticulture from Clemson University. Drawing on her years of ministry as a Bible teacher, she combines her knowledge of horticulture with rich biblical truths to help others become rooted in Christ, cultivate joy, and sow grace. She has worked at local garden centers, taught gardening workshops and classes, and worked as a garden consultant and designer.

As a writer and speaker, she has over thirty years of ministry experience and is a pastor's wife and Bible teacher. As a writer, she writes devotions and articles for a variety of publications. She has been published in anthologies, and several of her stories have appeared in the Chicken Soup for the Soul book series. As a speaker, she speaks at women's events and conferences, and she also teaches at writers' conferences. Her photography has been featured in garden calendars and is now included in her debut devotional.

When she's not digging in the dirt or in God's Word, she's off with her Canon camera photographing gardens, landscapes, and sunrises at the coast. As for digging, one of these requires gloves, and the other doesn't, but both bring peace, comfort, and the joy of sharing her knowledge with others. You can connect with Beth at www.BethFortune.com.